Penguin 75

Designers,

Authors,

Commentary

(the good,

the bad . . .)

A Celebration

of the 75th

Anniversary of

Penguin Books

Edited with an
Introduction
by Paul Buckley

Foreword
by Chris Ware

Book Design
by Christopher Brand

Contents

Penguin 75

CONTRIBUTORS:

Title: Author | Translator, Scholar, Editor, Publisher | Designer, Art Director, Illustrator, Photographer

Penguin publishers:

Kathryn Court
President and Publisher, Penguin Books

Stephen Morrison
Associate Publisher and Editor in Chief,
Penguin Books

Some of these covers were originally conceived under
the Viking hardcover imprint or The Penguin Press
hardcover imprint. On their respective pages, these
covers are listed as *Adapted from the Viking hardcover*
or *Adapted from The Penguin Press hardcover.*

Clare Ferraro
President, Viking and Plume

Paul Slovak
Publisher, Viking

Ann Godoff
President and Publisher, The Penguin Press

For titles where two editors are listed, the first person is
the acquiring editor, and the second person is the editor
who worked with the author and art director on the
cover shown in this book.

Paul Buckley is an Executive Vice President Creative Director at Penguin, where he oversees the covers and jackets for eight imprints. Working on such a large volume of diverse titles allows Paul and his team to work with some of the best artists in the United States and abroad. This book is just a small window into one of those imprints and the talents of the individuals involved.

PB

Roseanne Serra started working in the publishing industry right out of college, working on trade tabloids and magazines. Having joined Penguin in 1989, Roseanne is a Vice President Art Director, working closely alongside Paul Buckley. She currently handles some book covers on both the Penguin and Viking lists and manages the jackets for the Pamela Dorman Books imprint. Roseanne loves the dual role of designing covers herself as well as collaborating with artists and designers outside of Penguin.

RS

Darren Haggar has been Art Director for The Penguin Press since the imprint was established in 2003. Prior to his work for The Penguin Press, he worked as a designer for Penguin USA. He relocated to New York in November 2000 after working as a book jacket designer in London for eight years.

DH

Foreword: Chris Ware

In my twelve-year-old world, Penguin books represented the promise of a really bad time.

I remember one in particular: a spring break (my first, I think, to register as such) with plans of bike rides, sleepovers, and running around outside all smacked down by a thick slab of orange slapped onto our desks—*A Tale of Two Cities*, to have been read upon the class's recommencement. I won't detail the Sunday night choking-down of Dickensian this-and-that that transpired before Monday morning homeroom, but the sight of yet more Penguin orange in my ensuing academic years only compounded the sour association. (Those who have seen the British documentary film *49 Up* may recall the scene of the stuffy prep school subject proudly seated before his trophy wall of orange-spined Penguin books—it always gets a knowing laugh.) My aversion continued until my college years, when, suddenly and without warning, many of the Penguin spines were changed to a soothing sea foam green, and in the coolest of cases, a somber black. It was like Tums for a literary digestion still tender from its unvarying childhood diet: a simple decision by a veritable editorial genius brought Tolstoy, Flaubert, and Maugham out of the purgatory of pop-quiz acid reflux and back into my life. The lesson is simple: books, like people, aren't all the same.

As a graphic novelist, I fell into book design out of necessity, just as I fell into typography and printmaking. As a technical requirement of the style I'd chosen to tell my stories, I learned the work piecemeal, and probably poorly. Thus, the design-savvy reader should be aware: I probably have little idea what I'm talking about. It seems to me a book design should be inevitable—a book demands its own shape just as an oak sprouts from an acorn and a pine from a cone. A book is a body in which a story lives and breathes, and, like a body, it has a spine, is bigger on the inside than it is on the outside, and it isn't going to go on many dates unless it can hold up its end of the conversation. If it does find its way into our life, a book can also be a companion, and sometimes a life-changing one. Concomitantly, the book cover has evolved from a simple protective wrapper into something of a contemporary striptease between author and reader, both as a means of drawing attention to and selling the book, or amplifying and even extending the book itself into the reader's mind and fingertips.

As far as real book designers go, I've only met a few, but they strike me as thoughtful, well turned-out, and desperately cutthroat people. What surprises me the most is how shamelessly art directors rip each other off; a clever cover will sometimes be imitated as quickly as two or three months after originally appearing. Book designers, you should know, have to be ready to create something new, exciting, and original almost every day in order to eat, and a certain degree of burnout smokes out the weaker specimens; I can't imagine coming up with cover after cover without at some point resorting to an out-of-breath take, intentional or not, on someone else's great idea. This urge toward ever-freshness brings the profession perilously close to that of fashion, and the worst examples of such greet us at the grocery store checkout among the tabloids, gum, and ring pops. But the best of it, those that last, have recently been appearing from Penguin (yes, Penguin, not just the bearer of boring spring break assignments anymore!), following a path led by designer Paul Buckley into beautiful new ways of graphically proffering the written word.

Leafing through this collection of designs, it should be clear that whatever the focus groups say about book buyers and how they are daily dropping like flies, designers, despite their frailty, sure are a sophisticated lot. Where once typography and illustration used to collaborate to spoil a narrative moment before a book was even opened, type and pictures now operate independently, hinting at a disposition, a feeling, or a slippery state of mind harmonious with, or at odds with, a book's title (or the expectations that title might suggest.) Such an ineffable approach to design is much more in line with the higher aims of literature than it ever has been, and the methods are just as varied: a thousand-word-picture's worth of associations activate the flatly abutting images of Paul Buckley's covers for Don DeLillo, yet Greg Mollica's typographical palimpsests for Paul Auster disclose that author's penchant for narrative play in a world of letters. What I don't get, and I doubt the lay reader will either, is that even within all of the strikingly different and varied covers presented here lie branches and twigs of directions that seem perfectly good but were snipped or pruned in favor of more presentable (or saleable) shapes. Ron Currie's *Everything Matters!* is an especially dispiriting case of literally a dozen ideas being unaccountably ditched, the reader made privy to the ruthless rendering a book cover sometimes suffers.

But isn't a book, especially a work of fiction, ideally a work of art? As the reader peruses the anecdotes that detail each cover's creation, he or she should pay special attention to the degree to which each author's involvement and opinion shapes the final result. I personally find the relationship fascinating, having been on both ends of it, and being squarely in the camp that whatever the author wants, he or she should have. It doesn't always work out this way, however, and sometimes sensibly; authors are not always "visual people," but they might have an insight into a book's core that a designer might not. Some authors, of course, don't care at all and happily relinquish the reins. (I should add here that John Updike, whose knowledge of printing and typesetting informed his profession, claimed he could not begin writing a book until he first imagined its spine.)

With the current burgeoning of electronic media, the book cover may become less important as new ways of grabbing the reader's attention (short films, music, or god-knows-what) arise for as long as our power grid is still active. Some of these titillations may even evolve into reliable amplifiers for the ambition of literature, which will, I believe, never go out of style: telling secrets too subtle and embarrassingly serious to be said out loud. For the time being, however, for those of us who like our books portable, unchargeable, and printed, the following pages offer some of the finest examples I know of showing quiet respect for the general reader's intelligence.

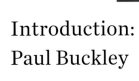

Introduction:
Paul Buckley

Publishers and editors are used to hearing art directors and designers moan endlessly about their best work being passed over by the philistines that surround them on all sides. They're also used to hearing from the authors about how there is no way the designer read the material and this lousy cover will surely bury the author's career. Then these poor editors and publishers have to gently navigate us through, hopefully to a good conclusion for all. Beautiful designs flourish. And massive book sales soon follow. Probably. Not really. Okay, sometimes. But never as often as we'd all like.

This being the case, design blogs are constantly asking, "Why does this cover look this way?" Often the designer appears online and diplomatically attempts to answer. But in all my years, I've only seen an author chime in once. So with this book, I thought it would be fun to get both sides on one page talking about one cover. And what I've learned is that when faced with putting their thoughts on the printed page, authors are far more polite than designers. But I've seen the e-mails. I've heard the responses. An author who dislikes his or her cover is often very *not* polite, and sometimes understandably so. They spend years crafting something that is immensely important to them, then we come along and in a matter of weeks, an editor sends an e-mail that is usually along the lines of "We are so excited to be showing you this cover! We hope you love it as much as we do!!! XOXO." (Really, I see the XOXO thing A LOT.) . . . and then major author panic ensues.

Who wouldn't hate something attached to an e-mail with two sentences, thirty exclamation points, and XOXO?

So why can't I get more than a handful of authors to honestly say in print what they hate about their covers? Maybe, I suppose, time heals all wounds. Or they get used to it. Are they just polite in print and designers are reactionary in and out of print? Probably. Designers are a passionate group, whip shy from years of constant rejection over work they truly try to impress us all with. We make terribly defensive husbands and wives, but we do have great taste. Seriously ... you should see the shoes I wear.

Who's really telling the truth on these pages? You decide. Enjoy, and thanks for buying my book!

XOXO,
Paul Buckley

01

100 Facts About Pandas

Authors:
**David O'Doherty,
Claudia O'Doherty,
and Mike Ahern**

Designer:
Gregg Kulick

Art Director:
Paul Buckley

Editor:
Rebecca Hunt

PB One of my designers was annoyed at me—so in an attempt to make nice, I offered her this book to design. Later she came into my office and said, "Why would you give this particular book to me to do?" "You don't think it's funny?" I asked. "No. It's ridiculous. REALLY ridiculous." To each her own. But to make someone do something she dislikes rarely leads to good results. So I attempted to give it to another on my staff, but she apparently already knew about this book, as the lunch discussion had apparently been "Why does he like this book? Or is he just trying to punish me?" She didn't want it either. Enter Gregg Kulick. . . . Finally, someone who thinks this book is as hilarious as I do. I hope it sells well, which might prove to the authors that Gregg's cover is indeed excellent. Better than their book, maybe!

Gregg Kulick
Designer

🖃 For a complex, panda-related masterpiece such as *100 Facts About Pandas*, I really needed to dig deep to truly achieve the vision of its authors. Many actors rely on a technique called method acting in order to become their character.

Method design is a similar technique that designers employ to become one with their graphics. I needed to know what it felt like to be a panda. Thankfully, I had a bible by which I would live my life for two weeks. I wore the same clothes, drank at the same bars, and even listened to the same music that pandas do in the wild.

When I came out of my isolation, I set forth designing the greatest panda cover ever designed in the history of man. Despite the clear masterpiece that was my cover, the authors were not convinced that it truly captured the spirit of the panda. My heart died, and I shall never be the same. I am a broken panda-man.

David O'Doherty, Claudia O'Doherty, and Mike Ahern
Authors

🖃 We said none of us like this cover. It's just not the right cover for our book. Our book is made-up facts about pandas, each one accompanied by a beautifully Photoshopped image. This should be the cover of a French children's book called *Peppe, Le Sassy Panda Napoleonique*.

They said, well do you have a better idea?

We showed them the cover of the U.K./Irish edition. It looks like a fact book or encyclopedia from the late 1970s. Cream and brown and beige with gold lettering, and a photo of a panda sitting at a computer in a bleak-looking office.

When they saw that cover, one woman vomited and another guy poked his eyes out, then shot himself because he was so bored. They said Americans don't go for subtle things like that.

We said many of our favorite things are American and subtle: Mitch Hedberg (comedian), Chris Ware (artist), Madonna (singer).

They said we want it to sell 50,000 to 100,000 copies.

We said surely we can come to some sort of compromise.

They changed the font. And got rid of the tongue. (The panda had his tongue sticking out originally.)

We said it's still completely so very wrong.

They said they had showed it to the salespeople and the salespeople thought it was a great cover. So great it should go into a book of Penguin's most awesome covers.

Crappy publishing jerks.

(Left) U.K./Irish cover; (Right) GK cover killed by authors.

100 FACTS ABOUT PANDAS

DAVID O'DOHERTY, CLAUDIA O'DOHERTY,
AND MIKE AHERN

02

The Angel Maker

Author:
Stefan Brijs

Designer | Illustrator:
Jen Wang

Art Director:
Roseanne Serra

Editor:
Kathryn Court

Proposed cover.

Jen Wang
Designer | Illustrator

🗩 The theme of the town's entwined relationships resonated strongly with me as I was reading Stefan Brijs's book. The novel is permeated with dark, evocative imagery that connotes a writhing mass of inescapable interconnectivity, and this is the visceral experience that I wanted to convey.

The snake in the initial comp for *The Angel Maker* was inspired by a description made by one of the characters, Rex Cremer, in regards to the main character, Victor Hoppe: "He was assuming that Victor possessed some measure of self-awareness, but that wasn't the case. It was much simpler than that, in fact—more logical. The answer lay in the snake itself. Victor was both the head and the tail. He devoured and was being devoured at once. That was it. He had no choice."

The snake in the form of a strand of DNA encompassed that idea of the Ouroboros on a thematic level, with the repetition of the past in the present, as well as Victor's cyclical fate, which draws in the people of the town of Wolfheim.

Stefan Brijs
Author

🗩 Hallelujah! Finally a designer who actually read my book! That's what I thought when I first saw this cover. At that moment, my book had already been published in many languages with as many different covers. The title, the theme of the novel—clones—and the gothic atmosphere caused designers worldwide to experiment with fluffy wings, endearing angels, disfigured faces, and giant ova, some human and some not. Dracula-like castles and threatening clouds on the horizon were also recurring themes. This cover, however, was totally different. Original. And for the first time, the content, theme, and mood of my novel were summarized in a single image, as I myself had also done in one sentence, somewhere in the middle of the final chapter: "If you draw a line, see, from here, the doctor's house, where the walnut tree used to stand, to the three borders, you can see how all the disasters seem to branch out from that spot, just like the roots of a tree."

"An exciting novel about the dangerous and tempting possibilities of creating life." —*de Volkskrant* (Amsterdam)

A NOVEL

THE

ANGEL MAKER

Stefan Brijs

03

Are You Ready for the Country

Author:
Peter Doggett

Designer:
Jesse Marinoff Reyes

Art Director:
Paul Buckley

Editor:
Jennifer Ehmann

PB Jesse has always been one of my favorite designers. His unparelleled knowledge of design history and his vast collection of ephemera always make for smart, uncomplicated solutions to any topic that has any historical significance—it will never be too loud, and we may not see it right away, but everything has a reason.

Are You Ready for the Country, full cover.

Jesse Marinoff Reyes
Designer

British author Peter Doggett's treatise on rock music with roots and influences in country and western (and the blues) was a chance to step back in time and reimagine when rock matured past simple, two-minute pop ditties and became structurally more complex and interesting—and in this case, reaching back to embrace its essential roots.

For me, nothing illustrated this notion more than the thought of Bob Dylan "going south" and recording *Nashville Skyline* (1969). The tricky thing was how to capture the idea of that, and not just a rote depiction of Dylan in the recording studio or posing for publicity. Ultimately it involved a little historical sleight-of-hand: Legendary photographer Barry Feinstein documented Dylan's 1965 concert tour of England, which included a shot of Dylan gazing out of the window of a moving train. A horizontal image, it would work spectacularly as a wraparound cover. Thus, the image was repurposed to represent the intellectual Dylan riding the rails to Nashville and the advent of another chapter in rock history.

Design-wise, I kept it stark, using a font suggesting old wood type—a condensed Clarendon, in keeping with the look of vintage country music albums and of "rural" graphics generally, farm catalogs and the like; and Cooper Black Italic, another old typeface that enjoyed popular use in the late 1960s. The "off-register" two-color printing of the rules and ornaments also suggested quick-printed catalogs or farm reports. On the spine I placed a pair of decorative framing devices to feature portraits of two additional musicians, Johnny Cash and Neil Young, to suggest the breadth of the book without having to get too complicated. Finally, we printed on uncoated paper.

Peter Doggett
Author

I first saw this cover in a bookstore in Denver, a year after my history of country music's collision with rock 'n' roll was published in London under different garb. It's a stunning photograph of Bob Dylan—other-worldly, enigmatic, removed—and a haunting cover design. But if I'd seen it before publication, I might have vetoed it, as it captures precisely the image that Dylan abandoned when he embraced the more conservative iconography of Nashville. The U.K. cover was more apposite, but less attractive. So: style or authenticity, which was more important? And that, ironically, was one of the key themes of the book.

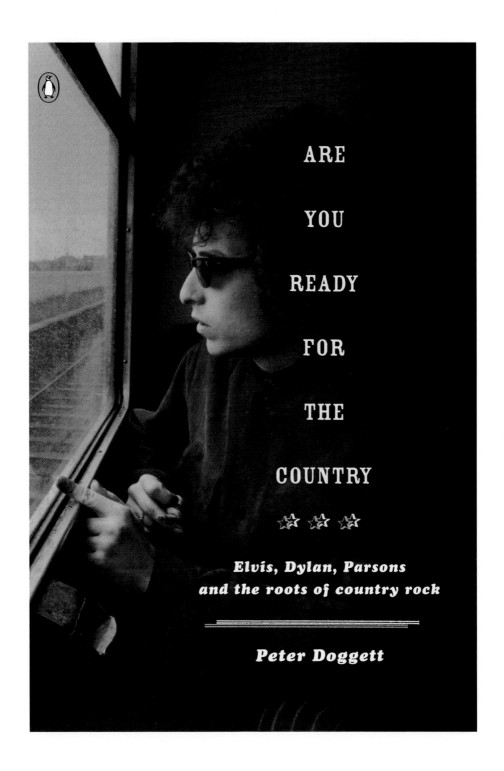

ARE

YOU

READY

FOR

THE

COUNTRY

Elvis, Dylan, Parsons
and the roots of country rock

Peter Doggett

04

The Art of the Tale

Author:
Daniel Halpern

Designer:
Paul Sahre

Photographer:
Michael Northrup

Art Director:
Paul Buckley

Editors:
Elisabeth Sifton /
Kathryn Court

Paul Sahre
Designer

As I recall, there were a number of studies for this cover that I was very happy with, each seeming to come into favor for a while with the publisher, but then falling out of favor once the author gave his input.

In order:

Color dots. Alternating color type. Clouds with purposely off-register type. Type made out of type, and so on . . .

In each case, I was attempting to create a cover that felt simultaneously like a collection of short stories that also felt international in some way. In retrospect, I think one of the problems with each of these studies is that they were trying to do too much. As a consequence, each ended up feeling abstract and unsatisfying

It wasn't until we hit on the idea of being super-literal and started playing with the idea of a "short" story that the idea for the final cover came about.

As a book cover designer, rejection is part of the process, but there are instances where the rejection—that to the designer might seem wrongheaded at the time—leads to a better cover in the end.

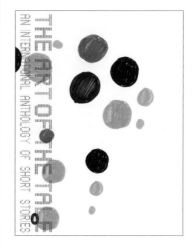

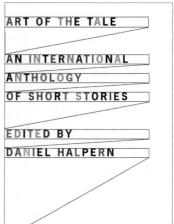

Proposed covers.

THE ART OF THE TALE

AN INTERNATIONAL ANTHOLOGY

OF SHORT STORIES

EDITED BY

DANIEL HALPERN

05

Paul Auster backlist

Author:
Paul Auster

Designer:
Greg Mollica

Art Director:
Paul Buckley

Editors:
Gerry Howard /
Paul Slovak

PB In my position, I get to choose what I will keep and what I will give out to staff, freelancers, etc. So when an opportunity comes around to redesign something as glorious as the Paul Auster backlist, no art director in his right mind would give that out. I cannot remember the circumstances now, but I must have been out of my mind busy. Whatever the reason, I'm glad it happened the way it did, as these turned out so very beautiful.

Paul Auster
Author

From the mid-eighties to the mid-nineties, I published ten books with Penguin. I had mixed feelings about the design of the covers: some successes, some failures, all in a hodgepodge. A few years ago, the estimable Paul Slovak decided to "repackage" the backlist with a uniform look for the covers. My only suggestion was to consider a purely typographical approach rather than use any images. The result far exceeded my expectations. Greg Mollica came up with an extraordinarily brilliant and elegant solution: a set of variations using a few fixed elements in different geometric and color combinations from book to book, making each volume distinct from all the others and yet unmistakably part of a series. In my opinion, it is a masterpiece of contemporary design.

Greg Mollica
Designer

I noticed a large stack of old Paul Auster paperbacks on Paul Buckley's desk one night. Immediately I was curious about said stack, being a big Auster fan. When I asked Paul about it, he gave me the answer I was fishing for: "We're redesigning our Auster backlist, why?" Before Paul could finish, I asked/slightly begged him if I could take the project on. Paul was a bit hesitant at first, but I think he said yes so I would stop whining. A nine-book redesign in total. Buckley suggested "letter forms as ART." Ummm, okay, free typographic solutions for nine Paul Auster covers?! God I love my job, I remember thinking . . .

Soon after their release, I was invited to Paul Auster's book party. When I saw Mr. Auster, I didn't want to say anything, but my sister approached his wife, Siri Hustvedt, and insisted I introduce myself. Siri, sensing my unease, took over and brought us outside, where her husband was speaking to another man in the shadows. His wife was so kind and introduced us, and I said sorry to interrupt, and the man in shadow says, "Oh it's fine, I was just leaving." He walks off and Paul Auster goes, "Good-bye Don DeLillo." And I thought to myself, well, that makes perfect sense.

PAUL
AUSTER

IN THE COUNTRY
OF LAST THINGS

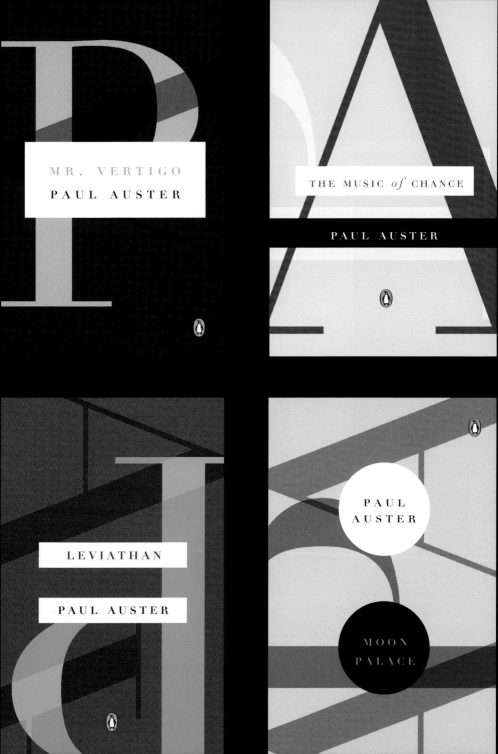

MR. VERTIGO
PAUL AUSTER

THE MUSIC *of* CHANCE

PAUL AUSTER

LEVIATHAN

PAUL AUSTER

PAUL AUSTER

MOON PALACE

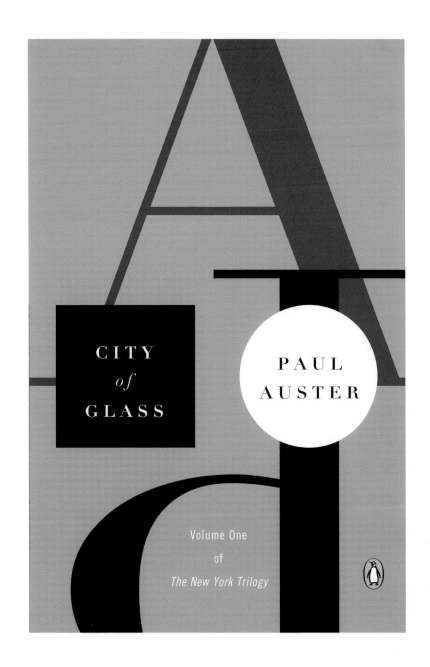

CITY
of
GLASS

PAUL
AUSTER

Volume One
of
The New York Trilogy

06

Bicycle Diaries

Author | Illustrator:
David Byrne

Designer | Art Director:
Paul Buckley

Editor:
Paul Slovak

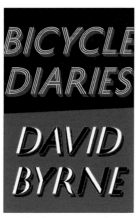

Proposed cover.

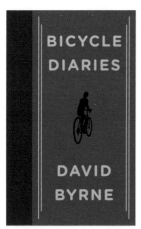

Viking hardcover.

David Byrne
Author | Illustrator

🗨 These things are collaborations based on contingencies and practicalities. That's part of the fun—it's a bit like puzzle solving. Having watched the still-recent evisceration of music packaging, it's clear that for physical books to survive, they have to be lovely to hold and view. The plastic CD cases are ugly things that fall to pieces—it's no wonder customers have abandoned them. Most books aren't very lovely either as physical objects—and one won't miss those either when they go.

I realized that not having a paper cover accentuated the books "objectness"... so, I submitted to Paul some jacket-less book samples and a drawing of myself on a bike. After a little research on the technical and pragmatic issues (blurb on back or inside? bar code on sticker or bellyband?), Paul came back with some nice layouts and type options, and we were off and running.

Paul Buckley
Designer | Art Director

🗨 David Byrne has done so much in quite a few art fields— we all know he's a brilliant musician and showman, but he's also a highly respected visual artist and has consistently made sure that everything that bears his name has been designed spectacularly. So having David Byrne come into your office to discuss his cover is pretty cool but also sort of daunting.

David came well-prepared with some bicycle sketches and a clear directive that he wanted something very simple. I was fine with the simple part, but I was a little leery of bicycle imagery. With the title *Bicycle Diaries*, using a bicycle on the cover seemed so darn redundant . . . and after we discussed David's sketches I did manage to politely bring up, "Hey, I did some all-type designs for your book that hint at movement indirectly, and that just happen to be right here on my desk. . . ." Working on them that week, I had convinced myself David might like them because of things I've seen of his in the past. They were loud and energetic and I thought "very David BYRNE." I was very wrong. He looked at them and quietly said, "I see, hmm . . ." a few times too many—and so to put us both out of our misery, I said, "So okay, you'll JPEG the finished bike drawing when you're done?" and he said, "Yes, sure, sure. . . ." And that was that. Comps meet recycling bin.

In the end, I went only one round with a cleaner design and we were both very pleased with the straightforward bold simplicity of the final cover. And though I still believe it's most interesting to depict a book's content, cover-wise, from a slightly crooked path, this one really works—David's charming drawing really pulled it together.

BICYCLE
DIARIES

DAVID
BYRNE

07

The Book of Imaginary Beings

Author:
Jorge Luis Borges

Designer:
Jesse Marinoff Reyes

Illustrator:
Peter Sís

Art Director:
Paul Buckley

Editor:
Michael Millman

Jesse Marinoff Reyes
Designer

When it was determined that the art should be rendered by the wonderfully appropriate Edward Gorey, the thought made me giddy (not a state I normally inhabit). I'd loved Gorey's art for years and collected both his extant work for New York publishers—including the cover designs he did in the 1950s and 1960s for Anchor Books—as well as his rare, self-published, signed-and-numbered issues for the venerable Gotham Book Mart. While the contracts were being signed, I had begun discussing cover ideas with Gorey and setting up a schedule. In the midst of this, in less than a week, Gorey passed away.

Years later, the book's editor, Michael Millman—having kept *The Book of Imaginary Beings* on the shelf—brought it back with a new and equally appropriate artist, Peter Sís. The Czechoslovakian émigré Sís was well-known for illustrating award-winning children's books, many with folkloric themes. Though not as macabre as Gorey, Sís's work had the same sweetness combined with a darker edge, giving it surprising power.

I approached this cover as if it had been a long-lost volume. The background art for the cover, spine, and verso were created from distressed nineteenth-century decorative bindings, and I used a framing device to display the cover art and ran the secondary credits to match the gold inlay of the frame. The title and author type were from an alphabet scanned out of an eighty-year-old lettering book to give that typography a more singular appearance, aged and mysterious. Finally, the cover was printed on thick, uncoated stock. The entire project is an exercise in historical illusions. Much like the fictional creatures Borges had cataloged.

Andrew Hurley
Translator

Peter Sís was the perfect illustrator for Borges's *The Book of Imaginary Beings*, and we sweated while he decided whether to accept the commission! And the "antique" cover, with its scuffed-leather-and-faded-gold-leaf look, was perfect for this volume in Borges's oeuvre, which purports to be one of those medieval-to-Renaissance bestiaries with their delicious mix of science, fantasy, wonder, and—why not?—a dollop of dread. Just the sort of physical book, one imagines, to have been found in JLB's own library. (The piece of leather broken off the spine was genius!)

THE BOOK OF
IMAGINARY
BEINGS

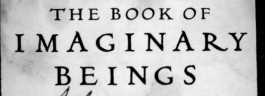

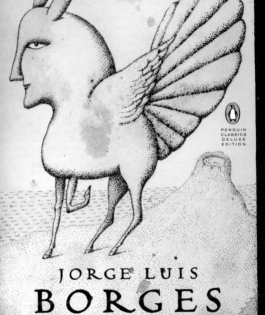

JORGE LUIS
BORGES

ILLUSTRATED BY PETER SÍS

TRANSLATED BY ANDREW HURLEY

08

The Breaking of Eggs

Author:
Jim Powell

Designer:
Gregg Kulick

Art Director:
Paul Buckley

Editor:
Stephen Morrison

PB This cover is classic Kulick, and its basic composition came about quickly enough—but as it was the sort of thing that would look good with any number of background colors, we went through quite a few and then finally settled on yellow. But it seemed every yellow we presented was met with "I'm sorry, it's just not the right shade." All total, we showed fifteen color variations till we met with an approval. I do like this cover, but the chosen color I feel is a bit washed out for my taste.

Gregg Kulick
Designer

It was a hot summer day, so hot you could put an egg in your pants and two minutes later have an omelet. No omelet today, though I already had a bagel. Besides, at 375 Hudson Street, the heat was just out of reach. July 22nd started out just like any other day—I woke up, ran my usual fifteen-mile run, rescued a kitten from a tree, and was out the door. But this day wasn't just another day. Another rush project for another late book. Out it went. Don't let the door hit you in the ass. Then it happened, my salvation came calling. I was about to begin the journey that would lead me to the place where I am today. The book was called *The Breaking of Eggs*, and although my name wasn't on it yet, one day it would be. This was no two-bit book.

Jim Powell
Author

I was dreading being presented with the cover for this, my first novel. What if I hated it? I was due to see it when I went to New York to meet my editor for the first time. What if I said it was awful? Would he still take me out to lunch?

Then this. It is magnificent. Dramatic, original, eccentric, and utterly true to the novel. I fell in love at first sight and have stayed in love ever since.

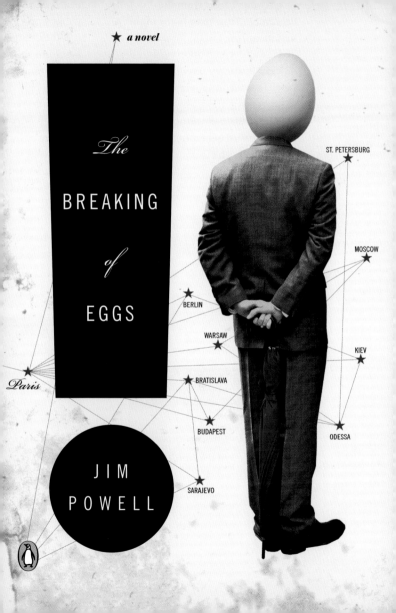

★ *a novel*

The

BREAKING

of

EGGS

Paris

JIM
POWELL

ST. PETERSBURG ★

MOSCOW ★

★ BERLIN

★ WARSAW

KIEV ★

★ BRATISLAVA

★ BUDAPEST

ODESSA ★

★ SARAJEVO

09

The Brontë Sisters

Authors:
Charlotte Brontë, Emily Brontë, and Anne Brontë

Designer:
Kelly Blair

Cover Artist:
Unknown

Art Director:
Roseanne Serra

Editor:
Elda Rotor

RS When dealing with our more special Penguin Classics, we are always thinking of how to create a special package, It has to be gorgeous, gifty, something you just have to have for its sheer beauty. I worked with Kelly Blair on *Jane Austen: The Complete Novels*. I wanted a gorgeous period piece that was also contemporary. In the end, the black silhouette of the tree gave the cover that darkness it needed without being depressing and took a traditional old painting and gave it new life.

Kelly Blair
Designer

🗩 For me, this was one of those magic jobs where everyone was in agreement right from the beginning. This cover is one of the first ideas I sent in to Roseanne, and it was decided upon very quickly. It was my favorite as well. I love that the full cover speaks to the three authors as well as the mood and place of the novels. I look forward to hearing how the Brontë sisters feel about the cover.

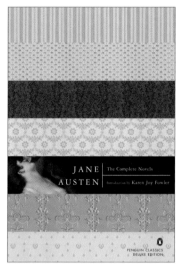

Jane Austen: The Complete Novels.

Juliette Wells, Ph.D.
Associate Professor of English, Manhattan College

🗩 Three sisters, each prodigiously talented but far from conventionally beautiful, are screened from the public world by pen names. Isolated together, they create works of fierce imagination side by side, in a gloomy house abutting the natural world, where they found solace and inspiration. Their originality is acclaimed and despised in equal measure by their contemporaries, who feared such passion in young women. Knowing how soon the shadow of death would fall on them all, who would not prefer to imagine the sisters as portrayed here: a trio of lovely women whose gaze speaks of genius.

The Bronte Sisters, full cover.

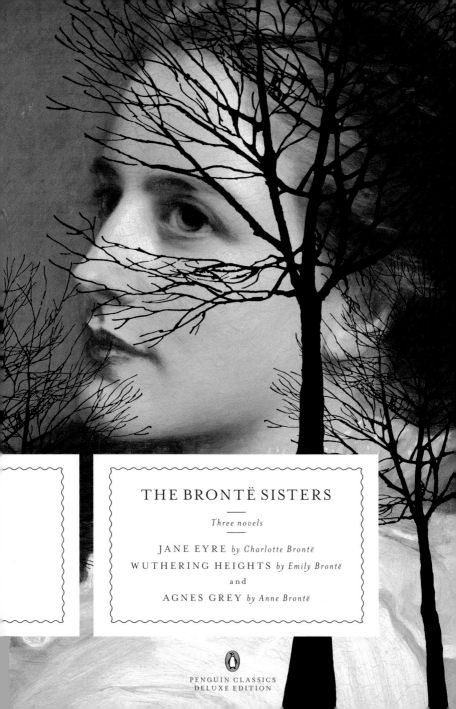

THE BRONTË SISTERS

Three novels

JANE EYRE *by Charlotte Brontë*

WUTHERING HEIGHTS *by Emily Brontë*

and

AGNES GREY *by Anne Brontë*

PENGUIN CLASSICS
DELUXE EDITION

10

The Broom of the System

Author:
David Foster Wallace

Designer | Illustrator:
Jamie Keenan

Art Director:
Paul Buckley

Editors:
**Gerry Howard /
Lucia Watson**

Paul Buckley
Art Director

🗩 This cover is a bit creepy when you consider that Jayne Mansfield was widely believed to have been decapitated. This turned out to be urban legend, but she did die due to massive head trauma when her car ran into, and under, the rear of a tractor trailer, killing all three adults up front. Following this unfortunate incident, all tractor trailers were required to install that low metal bar we see on trucks, the one that keeps us from going under the truck should we ever find ourselves in a similar situation. This bar is known as a Mansfield bar.

Jamie Keenan
Designer | Illustrator

🗩 *The Broom of the System* takes place in a Cleveland suburb, which has been planned to look, from the air, like Jayne Mansfield. That's all I needed to know. . . .

DAVID FOSTER WALLACE

AUTHOR OF *INFINITE JEST*

The Broom of the System

"Daring, hilarious...a zany picaresque adventure of a contemporary
America run amok." —*THE NEW YORK TIMES*

11

The Buddha of Suburbia

Author:
Hanif Kureishi

Designer:
Darren Haggar

Art Director:
Paul Buckley

Editors:
Nan Graham /
Jennifer Ehmann

Hanif Kureishi
Author

When it comes to the covers of my books, I prefer to leave the choice to the editor and publisher in whichever country it is. For *The Buddha of Suburbia*, when I think of how many covers there are around the world, I'm amazed at how different they are from each other. I wouldn't want to choose the cover because the editors would know better than I do about their market, about their readership. However, this is a spirited and beautiful cover. The type hints at something loud and bright, something waiting to bloom. For me it sits alongside the Peter Blake Faber & Faber cover. As I've only just seen this edition and it was published so long ago, I'm still getting used to it, but I'd say it's one of my favorites.

Darren Haggar
Designer

This is what's known in the trade as a "silent repackage." The cover is completely redesigned and printed the next time the book is due to reprint. There's no fanfare, no coverage in the catalog, not so much as a murmur about it. To be honest, I'm not sure this cover exists in the real world. I've not seen it in bookstores, not seen flat proofs here in the office, and I can't seem to locate any of the digital files (a little worrying if we need to make a change!). Looking at the cover now, I wish I'd done more with the type—perhaps made it look a little off-register to match the cover art.

Author of *My Beautiful Laundrette*

HANIF KUREISHI

THE BUDDHA OF SUBURBIA

"Raunchily, scabrously
brilliant . . . fascinating and
infuriating . . . Kureishi has
an extraordinary gift for
creating vivid characters."
—THE BOSTON GLOBE

12

Cheap

Author:
Ellen Ruppel Shell

Designer:
Ben Wiseman

Art Director:
Darren Haggar

Editor:
Eamon Dolan

Ellen Ruppel Shell
Author

🗩 I was walking down the street, carrying a copy of *Cheap*, and a neighbor—who happens to be a designer of, among other things, book covers—stopped me for a chat. This neighbor has known me for years through my kids but had no idea what I did for a living. He asked about my daughters, then about the book in my hand—was it any good? I said I hoped it was because I had written it. Surprised, he asked if he could have a look, and I handed it over. He turned it in his hands and said, "Someone put a lot of thought into this cover," and proceeded to explain why *Cheap* was such a stunning example of cover design. I listened appreciatively, secretly hoping he would ask me about the nature of the work captured between those covers.

He did not. But the following week he dropped by to say he had bought copies of *Cheap* for himself and a couple of friends. Evidence that you can indeed SELL a book by its cover.

Ben Wiseman
Designer

🗩 *Props*: $0.01
Scanner: $149.99
Adobe Creative Suite: $575.00
3 cups of coffee: $6.85
4 Diet Cokes: $4.00
Eyedrops: $3.97
Advil: $7.99
Wireless Internet: Stolen
Making it into Paul Buckley's book: Priceless

¢HEAP

The High Cost of Discount Culture

ELLEN RUPPEL SHELL

n Press hardcover.

#13

The China Lover

Author:
Ian Buruma

Designer:
Tal Goretsky

Illustrator:
Unknown

Art Director:
Darren Haggar

Editor:
Laura Stickney

Ian Buruma
Author

💬 A good cover is not an illustration. It conveys the atmosphere, the smell, the color, the feeling of the story inside. Gabriele Wilson's design below does this superbly.

The atmosphere of the young woman in the Chinese poster—an advertisement for something: cigarettes? a brothel?—suggests the allure of Shanghai in the 1930s. The girl's eye, artfully peering around the spine of the book, is knowing, seductive, a little dangerous.

It is a cliché, of course, but that is the point. The girl is a cliché in the way movie stars are clichés, endlessly reproducing images of themselves as brand names. Like the girl on the cover, the heroine in the book exists as an image, a mirage, a figment of the imagination.

Tal Goretsky
Designer

💬 After reading the first part of the book, I became obsessed with thirties movie posters, since the woman in the book is a Chinese movie star. I submitted the design below and prayed it would be chosen. As a precaution I also designed a version using the art Gabriele Wilson used on her hardcover design. That ended up being the final cover chosen. Turns out Gabriele's art was a photo she took of a poster hanging in her landlady's frame shop, next door to her office.

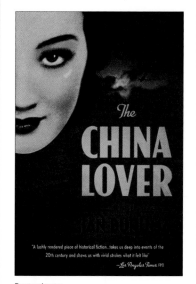

Proposed cover.

The Penguin Press hardcover.

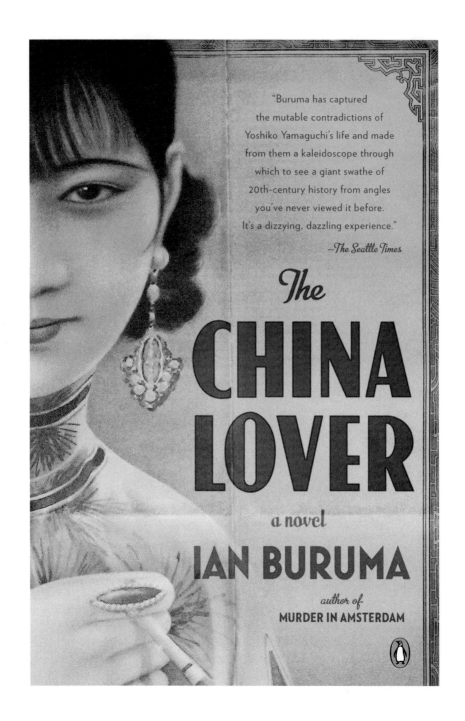

"Buruma has captured the mutable contradictions of Yoshiko Yamaguchi's life and made from them a kaleidoscope through which to see a giant swathe of 20th-century history from angles you've never viewed it before. It's a dizzying, dazzling experience."
—*The Seattle Times*

The

CHINA LOVER

a novel

IAN BURUMA

author of
MURDER IN AMSTERDAM

#14

Couture Classics series

Authors:
Various

Designer | Illustrator:
Ruben Toledo

Art Director:
Roseanne Serra

Editor:
Elda Rotor

Elda Rotor
Editor

🗨 When I heard from art director Roseanne Serra that fashion illustrator Ruben Toledo agreed to design all three covers of our Couture Classics (*Wuthering Heights*, *Pride and Prejudice*, and *The Scarlet Letter*), I was beside myself. As a student I used to cut out his illustrations from earlier incarnations of *Paper* and *Details* magazines, and had admired his murals in Barneys and his striking Nordstrom national print ad campaign. Although all three covers of these Penguin Classics Deluxe Editions are incredible, my personal favorite is *The Scarlet Letter*. Here we have a redheaded Hester Prynne in what I imagine as a cashmere knit dress with an oversized embroidered letter "A," the threads of which she's entangled. Ruben's depiction of the iconic wild child Pearl captures her in Issey Miyake–like pleats and a forbidding Anna Wintoury stare. How can any fashionista resist? But what I love most is that Ruben's cover bridges twenty-first-century fashion and nineteenth-century symbolism. I've seen early edition illustrations of *The Scarlet Letter* and was pleased to see the same imagery inspire Ruben Toledo, specifically the mob of chattering women, here spreading gossip across our deluxe French flaps, and the thorny red rose bush, creeping across the back cover. Finally, all font-crazed fans will enjoy Ruben's take on the letter A—the mark of adultery, in various serif and sans serif designs. Holy Toledo, indeed.

Roseanne Serra
Art Director

🗨 For the Penguin Classics Deluxe Editions, I wanted to explore a more feminine look. Maybe fashion. What a way to get young women inspired to read the classics! I approached actual fashion designers, thinking they would love to do this, but that became a horror. They envision things in 3-D, not print, they promise the world, and then they don't return calls. It was not pleasant. I had to put the idea on hold, but I really wanted to make this happen. Then it hit me. Hire fashion illustrators. They will get the idea. What a pleasure it was to work with Ruben Toledo and get his fun and crazed e-mails! This became one of my favorite projects after all was said and done!

Ruben Toledo (on *Wuthering Heights*)
Designer | Illustrator

🗨 *WUTHERING HEIGHTS*, MY personal favorite, it's such a BIG STORY spanning so many people—so much time, but all ATTACHED to this one particular place. I feel I HAD to DRAW the place—the GEOGRAPHY itself—in order to be true to the story. THE actual twisted landscape reflects the twisted story and people that live there in fact I believe that places do shape us as much as our DNA. The GLOOM and DOOM of the atmosphere is like an IMPOSSIBLE ROMANTIC GHOST STORY.

WUTHERING HEIGHTS

EMILY BRONTË

R. Toledo

Penguin Classics Deluxe Edition

Ruben Toledo (on *The Scarlet Letter*)
Designer | Illustrator

🗩 As far as *THE SCARLET LETTER* is concerned, what can I say—I'm a sucker for SEAMSTRESSES, as I'm married to one—I wanted to capture the ZEN-LIKE focus and intensity that I see in my wife, ISABEL's, eyes when she is embroidering or mending—the idea that women can WEAVE their own story, can SEW UP their destiny and try to MEND their lives is a captivating image to me, the idea that our children are forced to wear the HAND-ME-DOWN ideas of their parents—and at one point can SHED those ideas like an old COAT and be happy in their own skin. This idea of renewal, REJUVENATION, and rebirth is particularly AMERICAN to me.

Ruben Toledo (on *Pride and Prejudice*)
Designer | Illustrator

🗩 WITH PRIDE AND PREJUDICE, I wanted to capture the REVOLVING SOCIAL DIARY aspect of the tone here—it's like the DATING GAME, where everyone is supposed to be matched up IN ORDER TO win the game. . . . The writing style is superb, a great balance between the frivolous, flippant social whirl and some very heavy, underlying commentary on how some members of society, especially women, have to MARRY their way into freedom . . . or how some women are put into cages. THE black and white historical silhouettes help to illustrate the anonymity that can be facilitated by following FASHION, how by adhering to a certain style, you can disguise yourself and become a TYPE suitable for marriage and participation in society at large.

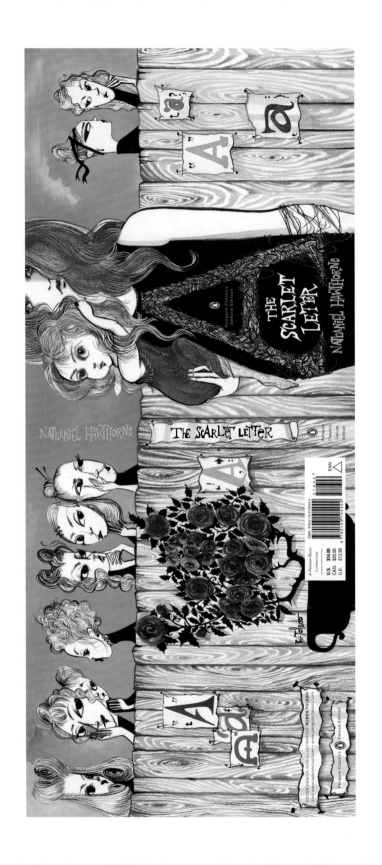

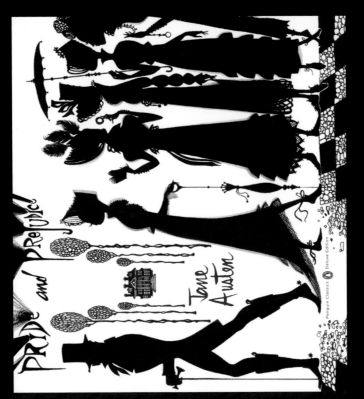

PRIDE and PREJUDICE

Jane Austen

Penguin
Classics
Deluxe Edition

Penguin Classics ⊛ Deluxe Edition

JANE AUSTEN ⊛ PRIDE and PREJUDICE

R. Toledo

EAN

A PENGUIN BOOK
LITERATURE

U.S. $16.00
CAN. $20.00
U.K.   £12.99

COVER DESIGN AND ILLUSTRATION: RUBEN TOLEDO
Visit www.vizbookclub.com • www.penguinclassics.com

Penguin Classics ⊛ Deluxe Edition

ISBN 978-0-14-310746-8

9 780143 107468

#15

Culture Is Our Weapon

Authors:
**Patrick Neate
and Damian Platt**

Designer | Illustrator:
Christopher Brand

Art Director:
Roseanne Serra

Editor:
Tom Roberge

Patrick Neate
Author

🗩 The cover has a slightly seventies flavor, which I appreciate. It doesn't echo other book jackets so much as the album covers of a less cynical time when genuine change seemed like a genuine possibility. If anything, the sensibility reminds me of Lemi Ghariokwu's landmark designs for Fela Kuti and Africa 70: bold and revolutionary for the bold revolutionaries—and, therefore, perfect for AfroReggae.

Damian Platt
Author

🗩 The haphazard way the letters are shaped reminds me of the construction of favelas, the layout recalls the work of Saul Bass, and the yellow and green invoke Brazil. The hand and the microphone are about being seen and heard, the essence of the book.

Christopher Brand
Designer | Illustrator

🗩 Normally, when I start to think about a book cover, the concept is the most important aspect to me. The idea behind this cover is very straightforward, but I think what it lacks in concept is made up for by the bright color palette and the custom typography. At first, this cover was one of my least favorite options that I presented, but it has started to grow on me.

CULTURE

IS OUR

WEAPON

MAKING
MUSIC AND
CHANGING
LIVES IN RIO
DE JANEIRO

PATRICK
NEATE
AND
DAMIAN
PLATT

PREFACE BY CAETANO VELOSO

16

Don DeLillo backlist

Author:
Don DeLillo

Designer | Art Director:
Paul Buckley

Photographers:
Various

Editors:
**Elisabeth Sifton /
Paul Slovak**

Paul Buckley
Designer | Art Director

💬 When I received the assignment to design Don DeLillo's backlist, I got so excited that I just started designing everything by DeLillo. When I brought this particular cover (below) to my cover art meeting, my publisher looked quizzically at my editor and my editor looked back at me. "Um Paul, it's gorgeous and all, but we don't own this book. Never have."

Jeff Brouws
Photographer

💬 Paul was very adept at matching the content and meaning of DeLillo's words to the visuals for these covers. I like to think that the tone of my earlier *Highway* photos (which Paul used) suggests the restlessness of an uncertain nation and communicates a foreboding, challenging the mythos of the American Dream and the underlying disparity so prevalent throughout our culture, despite the promise of economic equality and social justice for all. DeLillo mines these same themes and shows us the dark underbelly of things, the rotten structure behind the facade. As a big fan of DeLillo, I was thrilled that we two kindred spirits could merge our respective talents.

Jason Fulford
Photographer

💬 *White Noise* was my favorite book for a few years, so you can imagine how I felt when Paul asked me to work on this. I had just read about a controversial advertising campaign for the Bahamas. The ad's beach scene had been photographed in Jamaica. On the final cover for *White Noise*, the red slides were from Bucharest and the clouds were in Louisiana.

For *End Zone*, about college football and nuclear war, I shot my football falling from the sky. I used masking tape to add stripes to the ball, college regulation style.

Great Jones Street

Don DeLillo

Don DeLillo

WHITE NOISE

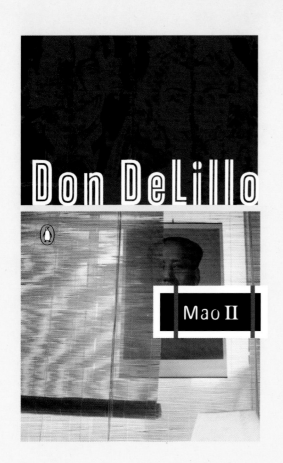

Mao II photos: John Vachon (top), Jason Fulford (bottom). | *Libra* photos: Unknown.

17

Gerald Durrell backlist

Author:
Gerald Durrell

Illustrator:
Mick Wiggins

Designer | Art Director:
Paul Buckley

Editors:
B. W. Huebsch /
Karen Anderson

Paul Buckley
Designer | Art Director

🗨 There are some people that art directors work with over and over, those rare few who seemingly do everything perfectly. Hiring them is so right and easy, and you know you are in the best of hands. Mick Wiggins is one of those guys for me. We've done maybe thirty covers with him, and I don't thick we've ever had one hiccup. These Durrell covers he did for me became instant classics of their kind, and his roughly twenty Steinbeck covers for our Penguin Classics line is an absolutely astounding body of work.

Mick Wiggins
Illustrator

🗨 I'm quite proud of this series of covers, and relieved. These covers had the problem of being just a little too juicy. The Durrell memoirs are dryly comic, replete with exotic animals all running amok in a private zoo.

When the subject matter is as rich and picturesque as these books were, it's difficult to think originally—and it's too easy to be lazy in conceptualizing.

And no matter the results, there's the aftermath. When there's a lot to work with initially, it's easy to feel afterward that one didn't quite make the most of the possibilities. There was, somehow, that elusive, perfect cover there, just ripe for the picking and within reach, and I somehow missed it. Again.

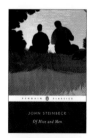

Steinbeck series.

GERALD DURRELL

Birds, Beasts,

and

Relatives

The hilarious sequel to the classic memoir

My Family and Other Animals

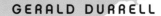

GERALD DURRELL

THE

Whispering Land

"An amusing writer who transforms this Argentine backcountry into a particularly inviting place."
—San Francisco Chronicle

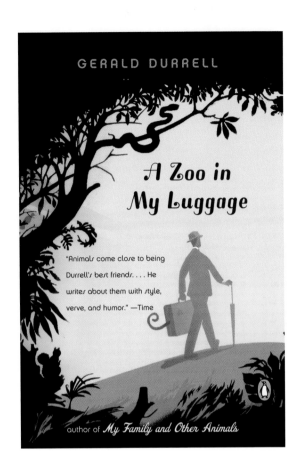

18

Eat, Pray, Love

Author:
Elizabeth Gilbert

Designer | Photographer:
Helen Yentus

Art Director:
Paul Buckley

Editor:
Paul Slovak

PB Often the visually simplest of things are the most difficult. Helen's styling of those three little words was nothing short of heroic. Suffice it to say, a ton of work went into this cover.

Helen Yentus
Designer | Photographer

🗩 Of course no one had any idea what would become of this book. There was talk of what a great writer Elizabeth was and what potential this book had, but really, who could have guessed? I could also say, had anyone known, I'm not sure I could have gotten away with this cover. I wasn't sure how I'd feel about this book when it was assigned to me, but as soon as I started reading it, I think I felt what so many millions felt. Here was a completely sincere, lovely, smart, and honest voice. I loved this book, and I did not expect to. So when the time came to design it, I really wanted to do something special. There was a lot of research done on the various places that Elizabeth visits in the story, but I could not figure out a good way to put it together. If I have to be honest, I cannot actually remember exactly how the idea for this came about. I had done a cover previously with some lettering made out of three-dimensional material and I think my art director, Paul Buckley, suggested I try something along those lines. All I know is that this was, in the end, one of the most difficult covers I had ever pulled off. The pasta and the prayer beads were difficult, but more or less okay. But the flowers were a nightmare. Each petal had to be arranged with tweezers. And really, did it have to be script? To make matters worse, this cover had to be shot twice. The first round of photos did not come out well. Needless to say, the flowers wilted, so I had to do it all over again. In the end, however, the time and obsessive efforts were worth it—I think it's the right cover for the book.

Elizabeth Gilbert
Author

🗩 When people first started asking me why I thought *Eat, Pray, Love* became such a phenomenon, I used to respond, honestly, "Because of the cover." I have since stopped saying this, because it sounds like I'm being dismissive or cheeky, but I still believe it. And I have evidence! Some readers have confessed to me that they not only bought *Eat, Pray, Love* because they liked the cover, but that they kept the book displayed openly in their homes for many months, for the same reason: They loved looking at it. I do, too. I cannot imagine this book with any other jacket.

ELIZABETH GILBERT

Author of *Committed*

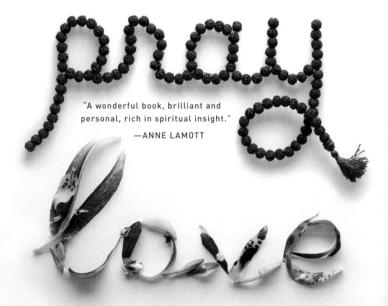

"A wonderful book, brilliant and
personal, rich in spiritual insight."
—ANNE LAMOTT

*One Woman's Search for Everything
Across Italy, India and Indonesia*

19

Emporium

Author:
Adam Johnson

Illustrator:
Viktor Koen

Designer | Art Director:
Paul Buckley

Editor:
Ray Roberts

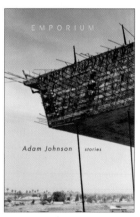

Viking hardcover. Designer: Paul Buckley.
Photographer: John K. Humble.

Adam Johnson
Author

🗩 I love Paul Buckley's cover for *Emporium*, the way our toothy child innocently skips rope, wind in her hair, school uniform on, sweetly at the center of a fish-eye lens. And then there's the bulletproof vest, which the reader only notices after. The first version of this cover had a boy dressed in forties attire, straight out of *Angela's Ashes* on a rooftop, sniper rifle in hand. I deeply loved the image, a timeless, classic schoolboy shockingly juxtaposed against the big rifle in his hands. But it didn't ring true with the book. The characters in my stories aren't out making havoc, they're going about their normal lives, foolishly unaware of what's about to befall them; and then there's the aftermath, where they often paralyze themselves or worse, overreact, making their daughters wear bulletproof vests.

Viktor Koen
Illustrator

🗩 It was the first time I met Paul, and he handed me the *Emporium* manuscript right there in his office as soon as I was done giving him my portfolio dog and pony show. Needless to say, I wanted to do well on that maiden assignment voyage and I didn't. We went through seven rounds of unsuccessful sketches, and when I was about to enthusiastically start working on round eight, Paul asked me, "Dude, are you applying for sainthood or what?" That's when I stopped, otherwise I would still be going at it. Though none of my images flew for the hardcover, a year later we found out that not only would one of my previously rejected images adorn the paperback edition, but that it was one of our favorites. There is justice in this world after all.

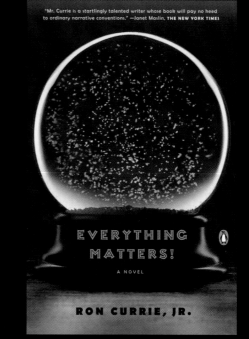

EVERYTHING
MATERS!|||

a novel

RON CURRIE, Jr.
AUTHOR OF *God Is Dead*

"Mr. Currie is a startlingly talented writer whose book will pay no heed
to ordinary narrative conventions." —Janet Maslin, **THE NEW YORK TIMES**

"Mr. Currie is a startlingly talented writer whose book will pay no heed
to ordinary narrative conventions." —Janet Maslin, **THE NEW YORK TIMES**

EVERYTHING
MATTERS!

A NOVEL

RON CURRIE, JR.

"EXTRAORDINARY"
"INVENTIVE"
"SUPERB"
"REFRESHINGLY YOUTHFUL"
"AN EXHILARATING RIDE"
"STAGGERINGLY AMBITIOUS"
"FUNNY, POIGNANT, AND TRAGIC"
"DAMN FUNNY"
"JOLTINGLY FUNNY"
"HIGHLY AFFECTING"

RON CURRIE, Jr.
EVERYTHING MATTERS!
A NOVEL

"Mr. Currie is a startlingly talented writer whose
book will pay no heed to ordinary narrative conventions."
—Janet Maslin, *The New York Times*

EVERYTHING
MATTERS!

A NOVEL

RON CURRIE, JR.

Alternate covers. Designer: Christopher Sergio.

(Bottom right) Photographer: Steve Bronstein. (Bottom left) Photographer: Mike Aßlolo, Lettering: Michelle Taormina. (Bottom right) Cover artist: Josh Keyes.

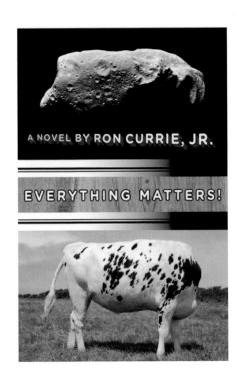

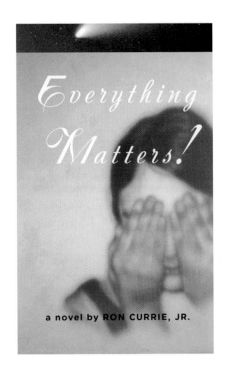

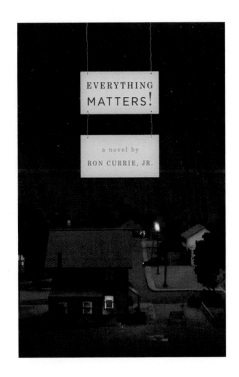

Alternate covers. Designer: Paul Buckley.

(Top left) Photograph of asteroid: StockTrek; Photograph of cow: Ashley Jouhar. (Top right) Cover artist: Kenichi Hoshine. (Bottom left) Cover artist: Paul Buckley. (Bottom right) Cover artist: Amy Bennet.

The First Word

Author:
Christine Kenneally

Designer:
Greg Mollica

Illustrator:
Nicholas Blechman

Art Director:
Paul Buckley

Editor:
Rick Kot

PB It's subtlety that is often the hardest to come by, and the most difficult to explain. When it comes to summing up a written premise with a quick visual, Nicholas is as smart as they come. This is just the sort of execution that someone unfamiliar with our industry might see and think, what's the big deal? I could do that. They couldn't, but the fact that some might see this drawing as being that simple is exactly what makes it so brilliant.

Christine Kenneally
Author

I didn't know what a good cover for *The First Word* would look like, but I knew what it wouldn't look like. "Please," I asked my editor, Rick Kot, "could we not have a chimpanzee or a mouth." Typically, books about human evolution have a chimpanzee or two gazing meaningfully at the camera, and many books to do with language have mouths. Not lipsticked, lush, irresistible lips but normal human mouths, open wide, lips drawn, speaking. These covers are particularly resistible. Instead, he sent me this cover. "Wow," I thought, "I want to buy this book." So did the hundred or so people who came to me after the book was published and said, *"The First Word?* Oh yeah, I saw it in the store. That's the book with the fantastic cover."

Nicholas Blechman
Illustrator

The original title of this book was *From Screech to Sonnet.* I tried to make an association between something primeval (a SCREECH) and something sophisticated (a SONNET). Because the book was about the history of language, all my sketches involved lettering: a crudely rendered *A* transforming into an elegant *A.* Then I started playing with the cliché diagram of evolution (a fish turning into a mammal, turning into an ape, turning into a neanderthal, etc.) and hit upon this idea of a monkey morphing into an *A.* The idea was just a black and white sketch, drawn on a long flight to Japan, but Greg Mollica turned it into a beautiful cover.

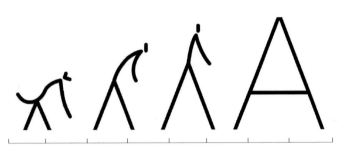

THE FIRST

WORD

The Search for the Origins
of Language

—

CHRISTINE KENNEALLY

with estates can
t of parameters,
ncourage a
ator to do their
about girls, guns,
was cool; he took
By adding lots of
e able to get it

Bond. I was baffled. Penguin U.S. hired me to do Ian Fleming's James Bond series. They seemed to be open to my ideas, but the estate had requested no naked women and no James Bond. *Casino Royale* would be the test. If that passed, I would do a couple more, and if they also met with approval, I would do some more, and so on until all fourteen were done.

Roseanne and I went through my sketches and picked one. We also chose a model to be James Bond (maybe if I shot him in shadows, unrecognizable, the estate wouldn't mind). With the help of my wife on hair and makeup, we photographed two models (for Vesper and James Bond) in my 300-square-foot studio apartment/photo studio. We also shot a friend for the Le Chiffre character and my wife and myself for the baccarat players. I then printed, colored, and composed variations to give to

Ian Fleming.

They didn't li

There was an
that was just rele
liked better. I kin
Those covers see
appropriate for J
slick, sophisticat
photographs inst
pulpy photograp

I was starting
I could rework it,
said it was okay, j
James Bond figur

James Bond d
some of them, bu
figure and as the
Walter PPK on th
Nudes made a few
toward the end, w
models were mor
estate seemed dis

There are nev
Fleming editions
James Bonds, bu
women. I like th

EMPORIUM

Adam Johnson   stories

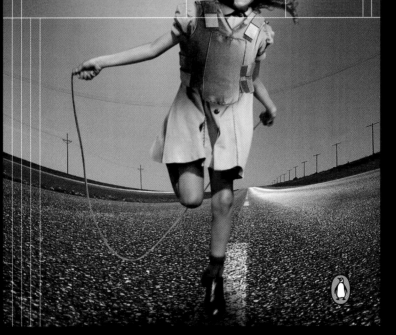

Paul Buckley
Designer | Art Director

💬 I'm a big fan of Adam's books and of Adam himself, as he enjoys having fun with his writing and his covers. I've met plenty of authors who take pains to project this sort of easygoing, let's-just-see-what-you-come-up-with-have-fun-go-for-it attitude, only to see panicky analytical floodgates burst open at the first cover suggestion; but when you meet Adam, you know immediately that he really does want to have fun with it and not take it all too deadly serious—so working with him and his writing can result in things out of the ordinary. We did consider the sniper boy quite seriously, but the very same week that Viktor handed it in, there was a deadly school shooting and it just seemed in bad taste; our publisher, Kathryn Court, was pretty sure it would quickly turn off any potential book buyers. I really liked that image, but maybe Kathryn was right—in situations such as this where something never sees the light of day, we'll just never know.

Alternate Viktor Koen images.

Everything Matters!

Author:
Ron Currie, Jr.

Designer | Illustrator:
Isaac Tobin

Art Directors:
Roseanne Serra and Paul Buckley

Editor:
Molly Stern

RS This book was agony in getting an approved hardcover design. Then the book did not sell well, yet got amazing reviews! For redesigning the paperback, Paul Buckley kept talking about the comet. Hence the marriage of the two.

Viking hardcover.
Cover artist: Amy Bennett.

Isaac Tobin
Designer | Illustrator

💬 I'm really happy with this cover, even though it's very different from my initial designs. We went through many versions before I found out that I would need to incorporate about a dozen quotes. To do this, Paul suggested that I combine the quotes with comets. So the final version was a true collaboration, but one that went smoothly and resulted in the strongest cover I submitted for the project.

Alternate covers. Designer: Isaac Tobin.
(Shuttle comp) Photographer: NASA.
(Hand comp) Photographer: Thomas Northcut.
(Little Boy comp) Photographer: Chad Magiera.

Ron Currie, Jr.
Author

💬 The first proposed cover for the hardback of *Everything Matters!* had a lot about it I didn't like. It centered on a figure, presumably representative of the book's main character, who appeared to have his pants on backward. Looking at it, all I could think of was Kriss Kross, the nineties rap duo whose gimmick was to wear their clothes backward, which raised interesting questions regarding who buttoned their shirts for them and how they used the urinal. Not exactly what I had in mind for the novel. We settled on something else for the hardback, a good cover but not a great one in retrospect. But then for the paperback Penguin's art department birthed the little slice of perfection shown here.

Proposed hardcover. Design by committee.
Cover artist: Chris Silas Neal.

007 IAN FLEMING

A JAMES BOND NOVEL

Casino Royale

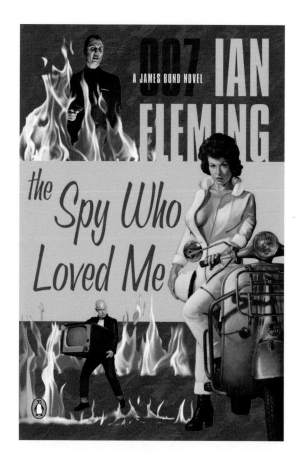

23

The Girls' Guide to Hunting and Fishing

Author:
Melissa Bank

Designer:
Alexander Knowlton

Photographer:
Photonica

Art Director:
Paul Buckley

Editor:
Carole DeSanti

PB Hats and gloves make great gifts this holiday season. For more thoughtful suggestions, see pages 38 through 46.

Alexander Knowlton
Designer

When the publisher changed the type of my hardcover design for this book to something I didn't like (below), I asked to have my credit removed. Biggest. Mistake. Ever. The book went on to be the biggest bestseller I've ever worked on and is now considered to be an icon of chick lit. I beat myself up for being such a prima donna until Penguin printed the paperback version as I originally designed for the hardcover and with my credit restored but modified: Cover design by a prima donna named Alex Knowlton.

Melissa Bank
Author

I loved this cover right away and went on loving it even after the art director said it looked like the cover of a J. Crew catalog.

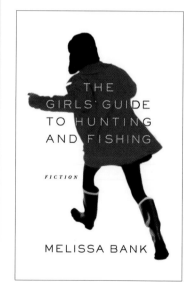

Viking hardcover.

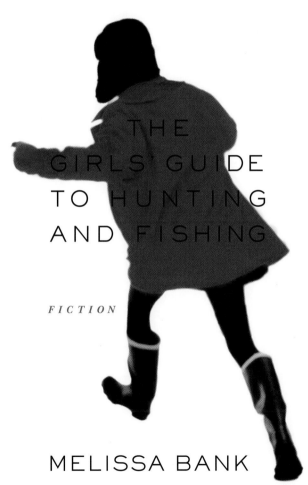

THE
GIRLS' GUIDE
TO HUNTING
AND FISHING

FICTION

MELISSA BANK

24

Candide

Author:
Voltaire

Designer | Illustrator:
Chris Ware

Art Director:
Helen Yentus

Editor:
Caroline White

Chris Ware
Designer | Illustrator

🗨 The history of cartooning is a troubled and embarrassing one. When the Swiss educator Rodolphe Töpffer noticed that a way of grabbing his students' attention was to draw little caricatures and picture stories relating to his subjects (not unlike, one supposes, the ones with which they were decorating their own textbooks during his lectures), he realized he'd hit on something, and from there, produced the first genuine comic book in 1831. He then spent the rest of his short life trying to live the thing down, insisting he wasn't a cartoonist but a serious literary man. The damage was done, however.

Then, 173 years later, when Helen Yentus asked me to do a new cover for the Penguin edition of *Candide*, I at first declined, recalling the annoyance and exasperation with which I'd plodded through the text in seventh grade while my English teacher kept assuring us students that it was actually a "funny book." I realized, however, that Helen was offering me a rare opportunity to speak directly to those seventh graders who now found themselves in the same dreary position I had experienced. *Candide* is, after all, a fairly dispiriting and hateful story—how many other books were we asked to read in high school where characters get their asses cut off? So I took all of these conditions under advisement as well as Helen's mention of my *McSweeney's* #13 cover as a model

(which had only recently been released) and was off to the races. I can't say it was lots of fun to do, rereading the book in a couple of different translations to be sure I "had it down," but in the process I realized that likely part of its appeal when originally published was the ridiculous speed at which events unfurl and tragedy repeatedly strikes (aside from all the philosophical pecking at determinism, Leibniz, etc.).

A few weeks after the cover was finished, Helen called to let me know that apparently the cover had found favorable enough truck among the people at Penguin (Paul Buckley in particular) that it was decided to begin a brand-new line of classics predicated upon it, each decorated by a different irreverent cartoonist—who, presumably, also hadn't paid attention in school. Imagine how proud old Töpffer would be now, his little teaching tool snowballing into a line of successful, respected literary classics. Determinism, indeed!

Helen Yentus
Art Director

🗨 In the thirties, Rockwell Kent's illustrations made this classic feel contemporary. I wanted to do the same with our edition. I immediately thought of Chris, who immediately turned me down. He was too busy, and I was heartbroken. Chris called the next week stating he had to do it, saying, "I mean, Rockwell Kent and me!"

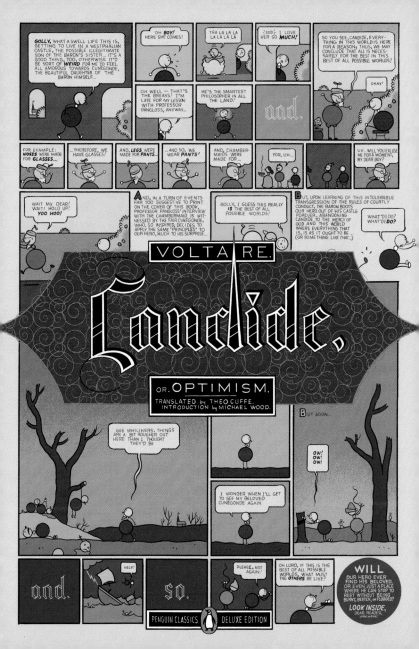

Philosophy in the Boudoir

Author:
Marquis de Sade

Designers:
**Paul Buckley
and Tomer Hanuka**

Illustrator:
Tomer Hanuka

Art Director:
Paul Buckley

Editor:
Michael Millman

Paul Buckley
Designer | Art Director

💬 *Philosophy in the Boudoir* is now a few years old, but still easily my favorite in this series. It's just so rude, lewd, and gorgeous all at the same time, and even though every time I commission one of these covers I tell my artists to "really go for it," Tomer made me the most proud in this regard. The one disappointment during this project was my associate publisher insisting that the horse's appendage be removed. I remember the conversation: "Wow, this is fantastic, but Paul, yikes—castrate that horse." "C'mon Stephen, it's the Marquis de Sade . . ." "I think you got away with enough here—be happy."

I am happy, but is the horse happy? A tad less so these days.

Tomer Hanuka
Illustrator | Designer

💬 The content here is hard-core, with revolutionary aspirations. Visually it begs for an aroused horse in a lavish living room. In the sketch for the back cover, the horse was juxtaposed with an image of de Sade choking a young woman. The front cover was relatively clean: one indecent gesture and half a nipple. Sketches were submitted and came back with mixed results. The horse would have to be castrated, but the nipple stays. Despite believing the penis is at the heart of the concept, keeping half a nipple on the front gave this illustrator a sense of finishing the project with nuts intact.

Pre-castration.

MARQUIS DE SADE

Philosophy in the Boudoir

INTRODUCTION FRANCINE DU PLESSIX GRAY

TRANSLATED BY JOACHIM NEUGROSCHEL

PENGUIN CLASSICS DELUXE EDITION

The New York Trilogy

Author:
Paul Auster

Designer | Illustrator:
Art Spiegelman

Art Director:
Paul Buckley

Editors:
**Gerry Howard /
Paul Slovak**

The Canterbury Tales

Author:
Geoffrey Chaucer

Designer | Illustrator:
Ted Stearn

Art Director:
Paul Buckley

Editor:
Elda Rotor

The Jungle

Author:
Upton Sinclair

Designer | Illustrator:
Charles Burns

Art Director:
Paul Buckley

Editor:
Michael Millman

Fairy Tales

Author:
Hans Christian Andersen

Designer | Illustrator:
Anders Nilsen

Art Director:
Helen Yentus

Editor:
Caroline White

Art Spiegelman
Designer | Illustrator

🗩 My friendship with Paul Auster goes back almost twenty years now, and we've found occasions to work together in small ways several times, beginning with a cover I did for his *Mr. Vertigo* in 1994. My cover for this special edition of *The New York Trilogy* let me emphasize the pulp fiction roots at the bottom of Paul's elegant metafictions. Thanks to my "enablers" at Penguin, each part of this trilogy got its own two-color frontispiece and I got to design four covers for the price of one.

Ted Stearn
Designer | Illustrator

🗩 I've always been hungry to see what I am reading. Maybe that's why I got into comics. So after reading Chaucer's vivid descriptions of all the characters who make the pilgrimage to Canterbury, I just had to see them—all of them! But the clothes were a problem . . . there are few images of fashion from the fourteenth century anywhere. Still, I was determined to have some authenticity to the dress, since the stories are so much a reflection of their time, and for some exotic visual flair. I ended up having to play fast and loose with the fashion, and not always sticking to the script. I hope it would be fun for any reader to guess who is who.

Anders Nilsen
Designer | Illustrator

🗩 I got the invitation to be a part of this project as an e-mail during a pretty heavy time in my life. I did the first drawings for it while sitting in the waiting room at a hospital, waiting for my girlfriend at the time to get called in for chemotherapy. I sent the final files just a couple of days before she died. In a small way it was a spot of light in a very dark time. A distraction, something to be grateful for. It was a cusp in another way in that it is the first book cover—the first proper illustration—I ever did. And it didn't escape my attention that I was, by far, the least well-known name in the roster of cartoonists chosen to participate. I was being placed, by strangers, on a list that included Art Spiegelman, Frank Miller, Chester Brown . . . It's quite a list. People I'd read with awe since I was a kid. Within a few months of finishing the job, I had severed my last dwindling ties to anything resembling a day job. And I couldn't have imagined a more perfect book to draw from.

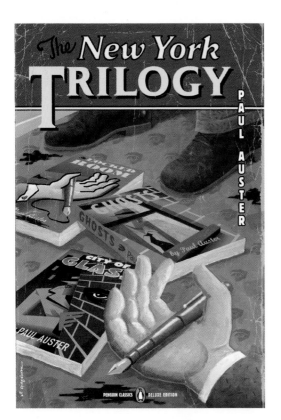

THE New York TRILOGY

PAUL AUSTER

GHOSTS

CITY OF GLASS

PAUL AUSTER

Penguin Classics Deluxe Edition

THE CANTERBURY TALES

A Retelling by PETER ACKROYD

GEOFFREY CHAUCER

Penguin Classics Deluxe Edition

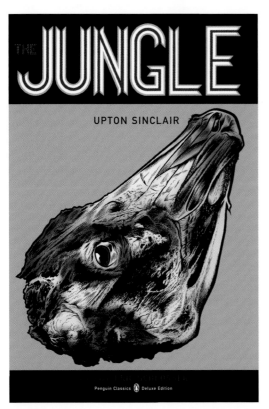

THE JUNGLE

UPTON SINCLAIR

Penguin Classics Deluxe Edition

HANS CHRISTIAN ANDERSEN FAIRY TALES

TRANSLATED BY TIINA NUNNALLY
EDITED AND INTRODUCED BY JACKIE WULLSCHLAGER

Penguin Classics Deluxe Edition

Cold Comfort Farm

Author:
Stella Gibbons

Designer | Illustrator:
Roz Chast

Art Director:
Helen Yentus

Editor:
Caroline White

Lady Chatterley's Lover

Author:
D. H. Lawrence

Designer | Illustrator:
Chester Brown

Art Director:
Paul Buckley

Editor:
Michael Millman

Moby-Dick

Author:
Herman Melville

Designer | Illustrator:
Tony Millionaire

Art Director:
Paul Buckley

Editor:
Elda Rotor

The Three Musketeers

Author:
Alexandre Dumas

Designer | Illustrator:
Tom Gauld

Art Director:
Paul Buckley

Editor:
Elda Rotor

Roz Chast
Designer | Illustrator

💬 I loved *Cold Comfort Farm*, and wanted to design a cover that would draw people to its cast of hilarious and peculiar characters, all of whom I could see quite clearly in my head.

I felt I was successful in bringing the characters to visual life. However, for me, once something is published, and it's too late to correct anything, that's when I see everything that's wrong. This happens every time I complete a project.

I wonder whether the other artists in this series have this problem. I would find it hard to believe, because to me, all the other covers in this series look perfect.

Tony Millionaire
Designer | Illustrator

💬 A few years back I realized that I had passed forty and never read *Moby-Dick*. I had read all of Patrick O'Brian's work, and I had built ship models so that I'd be able to draw a properly rigged ship in my comics. So I sat down and read it. I was surprised to find how funny it was—"I'll swallow a live goat with all his hair and horns on!" I forced myself through long slushy descriptions of whales and whaling. But what struck me most was the prose—"The starred and stately nights seemed haughty dames in jewelled velvets, nursing at home in lonely pride, the memory of their absent conquering Earls, the golden helmeted suns."

Helen Yentus
Art Director

💬 The comic classics became a really fun project to work on. Paul and I got to work with some of our favorite cartoonists on some great books. Dream job, really. Our real job became finding the right artist for each classic. On *Cold Comfort Farm*, Roz was obviously the person to work with—she would call me a couple of times a week and read me excerpts of the the book she found particularly hilarious. This is still one of my favorites.

Tom Gauld
Designer | Illustrator

💬 I originally submitted a much more reverential rough idea based on a scene where the musketeers fight some soldiers in a graveyard. I liked it, but Paul said I ought to have more fun with it and make something more me. I left it for a bit (I always sulk for a while when my roughs get turned down) and then had the idea of inventing a quiet scene before one of d'Artagnan's many duels. I didn't think that Penguin or the translator would go for it as it makes d'Artagnan out to be quite foolish, but that's how I felt about him, so I was glad when it was accepted.

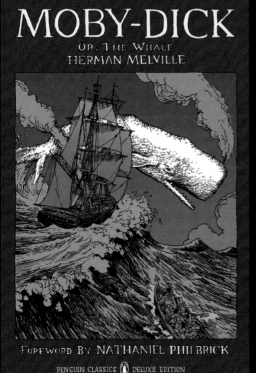

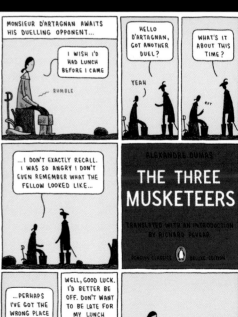

The Portable Dorothy Parker

Author:
Dorothy Parker

Designer | Illustrator:
Seth

Art Director:
Paul Buckley

Editor:
Michael Millman

**One Flew Over
the Cuckoo's Nest**

Author:
Ken Kesey

Designer | Illustrator:
Joe Sacco

Art Director:
Paul Buckley

Editors:
Phyllis Levy /
Paul Slovak

Gravity's Rainbow

Author:
Thomas Pynchon

Illustrator:
Frank Miller

Designer | Art Director:
Paul Buckley

Editors:
Corlies Smith /
Ann Godoff

Revolutionary Suicide

Author:
Huey P. Newton

Designer | Illustrator:
Che Anderson

Art Director:
Paul Buckley

Editor:
Elda Rotor

Seth
Designer | Illustrator:

💬 When Paul Buckley called me up for the Penguin Classics line and offered me *The Portable Dorothy Parker*, I was pleased. I have always loved Dorothy Parker, and it was a good fit. But a thought crossed my mind. Maybe it was TOO GOOD of a fit. I am often thought of as having a *NEW YORKER*ish drawing style—often asked to do drawings to accompany witty or urbane works. Maybe it might be a good idea to shake things up and take on an author that would be more at odds with my work. So I asked Paul, "I love Dorothy Parker, she'd be a joy to do but . . . who else have you got?" Pause. Paul's stony reply was, "Dorothy Parker." Pause. My quick answer: "Dorothy Parker sounds great to me—let's do it."

Right away, I knew I should try to use the various surfaces of the jacket (front, spine, back, and flaps) to give some sense of Dottie's life and work. And I wanted it to be light but not to shy away from the darker elements of her persona. I pulled out Margaret Mead's biography (*What Fresh Hell Is This?*)—which I had read more than a decade before—and quickly pored over it for a refresher course. Between that and her poetry, I pretty much had all the elements I needed for the covers. I hoped to transmit some of her wonderfully acerbic, witty personality but also to hint at her pain as well. It was a godsend that much of her verse is short because

it allowed me to use full poems in tiny spaces. I chose a big face for the cover, which is a pretty boring idea, really, because I knew there would be so much visual clutter on the back and flaps that it would need a strong central image to give the whole package some focus. And let's face it, for a book of Dorothy Parker—you want to see Dorothy Parker front and center.

I genuinely enjoyed working on the book. A great opportunity to link myself, however peripherally, to such a marvelous writer. And, of course, I immensely enjoyed reimmersing myself in Parker's writing. Especially "Big Blonde." A little masterpiece.

Joe Sacco
Designer | Illustrator

💬 My priority with drawing the cover for *One Flew Over the Cuckoo's Nest* was to get the movie version and especially Jack Nicholson's face out of my mind. I reread the book, which was an enormous pleasure, and the solution was in front of me. The main protagonist, as Kesey described him, looked nothing like Mr. Nicholson. I simply followed Kesey's directions to get a big-jawed, redheaded McMurphy. The other thing about the cover assignment that still makes me feel warm is that now my name is forever tied, even tangentially, to Ken Kesey's.

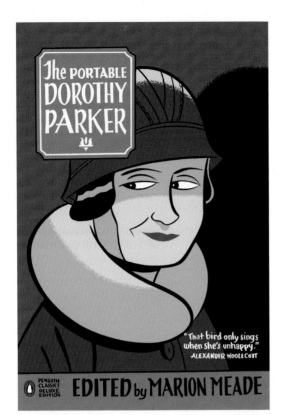

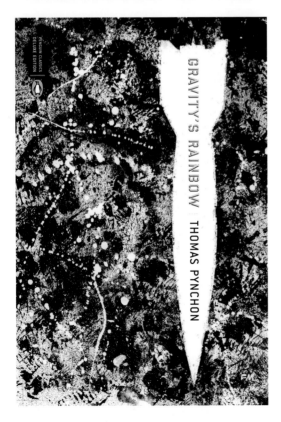

Ethan Frome

Author:
Edith Wharton

Designer | Illustrator:
Jeffrey Brown

Art Director:
Paul Buckley

Editor:
Elda Rotor

The Adventures of Huckleberry Finn

Author:
Mark Twain

Illustrator:
Lilli Carre

Designer | Art Director:
Paul Buckley

Editor:
Elda Rotor

The Dharma Bums

Author:
Jack Kerouac

Designer | Illustrator:
Jason Lambiek

Art Director:
Paul Buckley

Editors:
Malcolm Cowley /
Paul Slovak

White Noise

Author:
Don DeLillo

Illustrator:
Michael Cho

Designer | Art Director:
Paul Buckley

Editors:
Elisabeth Sifton /
Paul Slovak

Lilli Carre
Illustrator

🗩 The possibilities of design and interpretation in the Graphic Classics series has allowed for some truly strange and beautiful interpretations. I think one of the best parts of the series is the lack of restrictions and the real estate of the entire cover, spine, and flaps—every little inch. The prospect of getting to make a new face for *The Adventures of Huckleberry Finn* for this series was both very exciting and very nerve-racking. The book has had many printings over the years, and I looked through lots of its previous covers, many of which were rather on the dull side.

In my final front cover design, I tried to get the wildness, risk, and attitude of Huck and the story into one bright image. Many of the elements in the final design are split in two, quite literally with the water line, and the daytime on the front and nighttime on the back cover, and Jim and Huck hidden in the leaves on the alternate book flaps. I wanted it to feel both quiet and loud at once, much like the feel of the story itself.

Jason Lambiek
Designer | Illustrator

🗩 Aahh, I always hated this part in art school! Well, here goes:

I didn't want to do a comic strip as the cover for *The Dharma Bums*. I preferred to try to condense the book into an image that was as simple as possible, combining both the spiritual search and the bumming around part of the novel, feeling that would work best visually on the cover. The literary talks that take place in the novel would work better shown as strips on the flaps, the dialogue taken directly from within.

All text is handwritten, mainly because I don't own a computer. Hopefully, together with a minimalistic use of color, it gave the book a rough, handmade, and timeless feel that fits the content.

Michael Cho
Illustrator

🗩 *White Noise* is actually a favorite book of mine, so I was very honored to work on this cover. And I was actually reading Don DeLillo's *Libra* when I got the call for this assignment. Initially, I was a bit daunted because Paul gave me complete freedom to do whatever I wanted (usually marketing factors dictate some sort of design), but I jumped in and painted what, in an ideal world, would be the cover I'd want to see.

EDITH WHARTON

ETHAN FROME

PENGUIN CLASSICS DELUXE EDITION

The Adventures of

HUCKLEBERRY FINN

by Mr. MARK TWAIN

PENGUIN CLASSICS DELUXE EDITION

the

DHARMA BUMS

by JACK KEROUAC

NIRVANA

introduction by
ANN DOUGLAS

PENGUIN CLASSICS
DELUXE EDITION

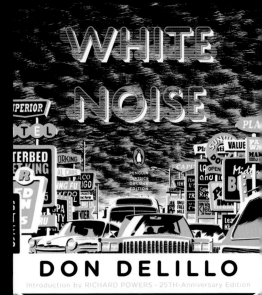

WHITE NOISE

SUPERIOR

DON DELILLO

Introduction by RICHARD POWERS · 25TH-Anniversary Edition

Little Women

Author:
Louisa May Alcott

Designer | Illustrator:
Julie Doucet

Art Director:
Paul Buckley

Editor:
Elda Rotor

Paul Buckley
Art Director

💬 Julie had the hardest time with this one. Or maybe, more correctly, I was the one that was not getting it. I kept asking her to really go for it, and she kept e-mailing back "but they are such good girls!" She was giving me sketches of girls holding bibles saying really nice things to each other, and word bubbles like "God is good" were in abundance.

I hired Julie for this particular title because . . . well, I'd rather not describe in print the things I've seen her draw . . . Google image "Julie Doucet" (turn SafeSearch to off) and you'll see what I mean—Julie gets really REALLY DARK, and I thought she'd turn this book on its head. At the end of the day, though, the book is what it is, and the most we could do was to make light mention of boys. I insisted on pimples, though . . . lots and lots of pimples.

Julie Doucet
Designer | Illustrator

💬 Being French Canadian, I had never heard of Louisa May Alcott's *Little Women*. I had no notion of its social and historical importance. I read the book. I mostly thought it was boring and I was terribly irritated by its deep puritanism. Paul Buckley's instructions were to "give an edge" to the cover, to brighten it up, to make the book look fun. That totally baffled me, because I couldn't see anything even close to fun anywhere in it. Paul couldn't understand why I didn't understand what he wanted me to do. I really didn't get it. I did MANY sketches. And eventually I came up with something he was pleased with. But I still didn't get it. A couple of months later, I came across the wonderful 1949 Mervyn LeRoy *Little Women* film. Only then did I get it.

PENGUIN CLASSICS DELUXE EDITION

Rashōmon

Author:
Ryūnosuke Akutagawa

Illustrator:
Yoshihiro Tatsumi

Designer | Art Director:
Helen Yentus

Editor:
Michael Millman

Frankenstein

Author:
Mary Shelley

Designer | Illustrator:
Daniel Clowes

Art Director:
Paul Buckley

Editor:
John Siciliano

We Have Always Lived in the Castle

Author:
Shirley Jackson

Designer | Illustrator:
Thomas Ott

Art Director:
Herb Thornby

Editor:
Caroline White

Metamorphosis

Author:
Franz Kafka

Designer | Illustrator:
Sammy Harkham

Art Director:
Paul Buckley

Editor:
John Siciliano

Yoshihiro Tatsumi
Illustrator

🗩 The author is Ryūnosuke Akutagawa, one of the great writers in Japanese history. The introduction is by Haruki Murakami, the most popular Japanese author of today. And the film version was made by the noted director Akira Kurosawa.

I was honored, but I struggled with this when Penguin Books commissioned me to paint a cover for *Rashōmon*.

I am told that this year is the seventy-fifth anniversary of Penguin Books. I am seventy-five years old this year. Congratulations to Penguin Books! And to me, too!

Thomas Ott
Designer | Illustrator

🗩 I'm not a person who tries to make contacts all over the world to get work. So when Penguin Books contacted me, I was very surprised.

To me, even in a modern world, the U.S. still seems to be so far away from Switzerland.

I was impressed by the beautiful covers other illustrators did for this collection and that I had the opportunity to collaborate on one.

So I agreed with a lot of optimism, read Shirley Jackson's book, and tried to make something nice as well.

Personally, I'm not very happy about my cover now, as most of the characters came out a little stiff.

PS: I still wonder how they got my e-mail address.

Daniel Clowes
Designer | Illustrator

🗩 When I was first approached by Paul to do a cover for the Penguin Classics series, I was planning to wait until something really appropriate came along (I was hoping for *The Day of the Locust*) and wound up turning down several books over the course of a year or so. At some point during that time, I learned I was going to need open-heart surgery, and when I saw *Frankenstein* on the list, I thought it seemed like a choice that would perhaps have some resonance once I emerged from the fog of anesthesia. I had read the book as a teenager, disappointed at the lack of gruesome thrills, but this time I couldn't have loved it more, and not because I related to Victor's monster and his stitched-up torso, but more for the the queasy, dreamlike connections to my own recent parenthood and the way it captures the competing senses of loathing and tenderness one can feel toward his own creations (both "artistic" and biological).

Paul Buckley
Art Director

🗩 Being that much of my time is spent contacting the people I hire to discuss the latest nitpick or to navigate a complete rejection, this series has come to represent a true retreat from all that—a license to let talented people do what they do best, with little to no interference. The results speak volumes.

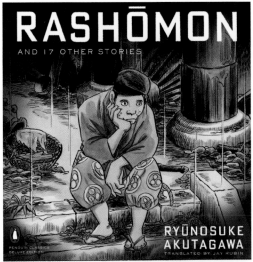

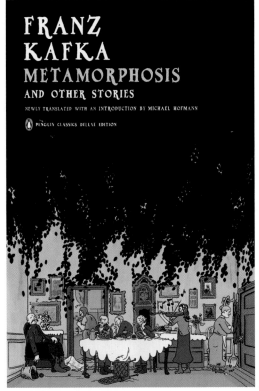

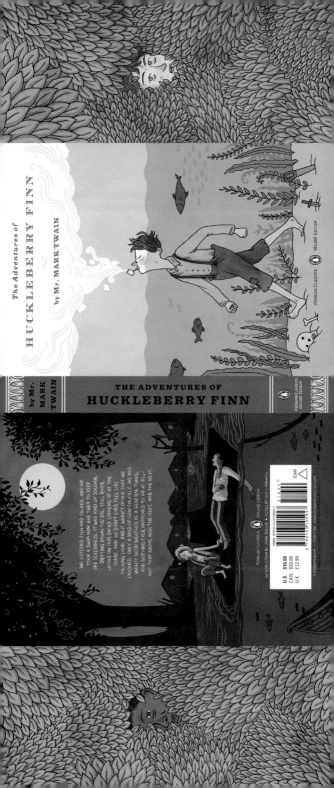

THE JUNGLE

UPTON SINCLAIR

THE JUNGLE

Upton Sinclair's dramatic and deeply moving story exposed the brutal conditions in the Chicago stockyards at the turn of the nineteenth century and brought into sharp moral focus the appalling odds against which immigrants and other working people struggled for their share of the American dream. Denounced by the conservative press as an American libel on the meatpacking industry, the book was championed by more progressive thinkers, including then president Theodore Roosevelt, and was a major catalyst to the passing of the Pure Food and Meat Inspection Act, which has tremendous impact to this day.

UPTON SINCLAIR was a passionate believer in the redemption of mankind through social reform. His exposé of the interlocking corruption in American corporate and political life was a major literary event when it was published in 1906, and caused an almost immediate reform in pure-food legislation. This edition includes a brand new foreword from Eric Schlosser, author of the bestselling *Fast Food Nation*.

A Penguin Book | Literature

Penguin Classics ⬤ Deluxe Edition

Penguin Classics
Deluxe Edition

Penguin Classics
Deluxe Edition

www.penguinclassics.com

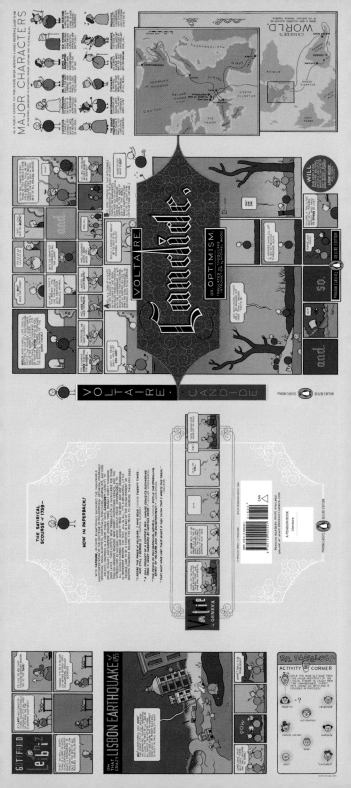

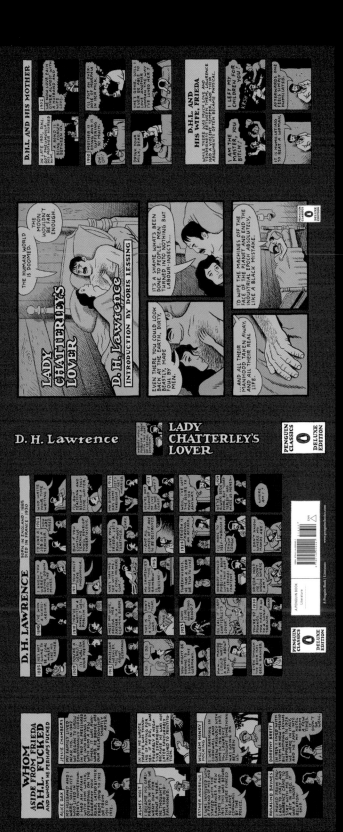

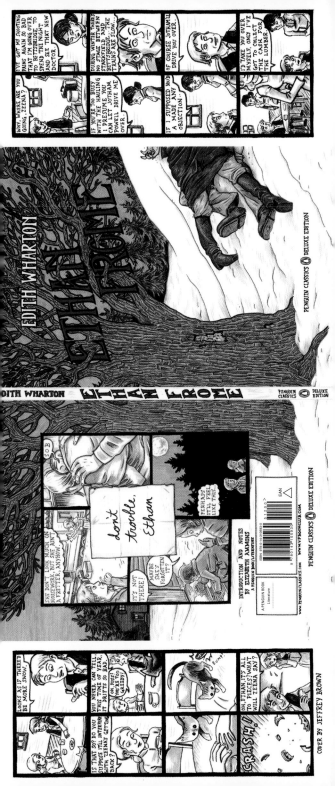

HANS CHRISTIAN ANDERSEN

FAIRY TALES

TRANSLATED BY TIINA NUNNALLY

EDITED AND INTRODUCED BY JACKIE WULLSCHLAGER

HANS CHRISTIAN ANDERSEN FAIRY TALES

A PENGUIN BOOK / LITERATURE   WWW.PENGUINCLASSICS.COM

"All right. Now let's begin. When we reach the end of the story, we'll know more than we know now."

HANS CHRISTIAN ANDERSEN WAS THE PRODIGIOUSLY IMAGINATIVE WRITER AND STORYTELLER WHO REVOLUTIONIZED LITERATURE FOR CHILDREN. HE GAVE US THE NOW-STANDARD VERSIONS OF SOME TRADITIONAL FOLK TALES — WITH AN ANARCHIC TWIST — BUT MANY OF HIS MOST FAMOUS TALES SPRANG DIRECTLY FROM HIS IMAGINATION. THE THIRTY STORIES HERE RANGE FROM EXUBERANT EARLY WORKS LIKE "THE TINDERBOX" TO ANDERSEN'S NEW CLASSIC OF CHILDHOOD INSOMNIA IN "THE PRINCESS ON THE PEA." THESE NEW TRANSLATIONS, BY TIINA NUNNALLY, ACCLAIMED TRANSLATOR, ENHANCED BY JACKIE WULLSCHLAGER'S CAPTIVATING INTRODUCTION AND ANDERSEN'S OWN PAPER CUTS, THIS VOLUME WILL DAZZLE READERS YOUNG AND OLD.

ANDERS BREKHUS NILSEN 2005

A PENGUIN BOOK
Literature

ISBN 0-14-303932-0
$11.00

9 780143 039327

EAN

SHIRLEY JACKSON

WE HAVE ALWAYS LIVED IN THE CASTLE

INTRODUCTION BY JONATHAN LETHEM

My name is Mary Katherine Blackwood. I am eighteen years old, and I live with my sister Constance. I have often thought that with any luck at all I could have been born a were-wolf, because the two middle fingers on both my hands are the same length, but I have had to be content with what I had.

I dislike washing myself, and dogs, and noise. I like my sister Constance, and Richard Plantagenet, and Amanita phalloides, the death-cup mushroom. Everyone else in my family is dead.

You will be wondering about that sugar bowl, I imagine. Is it still in use? you are wondering; has it been cleaned? you may very well ask;

was it thoroughly washed?

SHIRLEY
JACKSON

WE HAVE ALWAYS LIVED IN THE CASTLE

CITY OF GLASS

As a result of a strange phone call in the middle of the night, Quinn, a writer of detective stories, becomes enmeshed in a case more puzzling than any he might have written.

GHOSTS

Blue, a student of Brown, has been hired by White to spy on Black. From a window of a rented room on Orange Street, Blue stalks his subject, who is staring out of his window.

THE LOCKED ROOM

Fanshawe has disappeared, leaving behind his wife and baby and a cache of extraordinary novels, plays, and poems. What happened?

PAUL AUSTER

The New York TRILOGY

PENGUIN CLASSICS DELUXE EDITION

PAUL AUSTER

THE NEW YORK TRILOGY

PENGUIN CLASSICS DELUXE EDITION

SOME STREETS OF
MANHATTAN
WALKED BY PETER
STILLMAN and QUINN
IN PAUL AUSTER'S
"CITY OF GLASS"

CENTRAL PARK

The Tower of Babel

CATHEDRAL PARKWAY

91 STR.

5TH AVENUE

WEST 94 STR.

BROADWAY

AMSTERDAM AVENUE

COLUMBUS AVENUE

WEST 84 STR.

WEST 66 STR.

BROADWAY

WEST 57 STR.

HENRY HUDSON PARKWAY

Hudson River

WEST SIDE HIGHWAY

SECOND AVENUE

PAUL AUSTER

PAUL AUSTER is the author of The Brooklyn Follies and eleven other novels as well as two memoirs, a collection of essays, three screenplays, and a volume of poems. His work has been translated into over thirty languages. He lives in Brooklyn, New York.

cover by art spiegelman

MOBY-DICK
OR, THE WHALE
HERMAN MELVILLE
MOBY-DICK · OR, THE WHALE · HERMAN MELVILLE

FOREWORD BY NATHANIEL PHILBRICK

PENGUIN CLASSICS · DELUXE EDITION

MOBY-DICK
OR, THE WHALE

HERMAN MELVILLE

PENGUIN CLASSICS · DELUXE EDITION

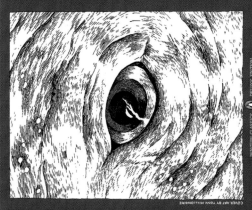

COVER ART BY TONY MILLIONAIRE

A PENGUIN BOOK
LITERATURE

U.S. $17.00
CAN. $21.00
U.K. £12.99

ISBN 978-0-14-310954-4

WWW.PENGUINCLASSICS.COM

To the Libertines

VOLUPTUARIES OF ALL AGES AND SEXES: IT IS TO YOU ALONE THAT I OFFER THIS WORK. NOURISH YOURSELVES ON ITS PRINCIPLES: THEY FOSTER YOUR PASSIONS, AND THESE PASSIONS, WHICH COLD AND SHABBY MORALISTS TRY TO INTIMIDATE YOU, ARE SIMPLY THE MEANS USED BY NATURE TO HELP HUMAN BEINGS AT-TAIN HER ENDS. LISTEN ONLY TO THESE DELICIOUS PASSIONS: THEIR SOURCE IS THE ONLY ONE THAT WILL LEAD YOU TO HAPPINESS.

LUBRICIOUS WOMEN, MAY THE VO-LUPTUOUS MADAME DE SAINT-ANGE BE YOUR IDEAL: TAKE HER EXAMPLE AND DESPISE EVERYTHING THAT FLOUTS THE DIVINE LAWS OF PLEASURE, TO WHICH SHE WAS FETTERED AN ENTIRE LIFETIME.

Marquis de Sade
Philosophy in the Boudoir

INTRODUCTION FRANCINE DU PLESSIX GRAY

TRANSLATED BY JOACHIM NEUGROSCHEL

PENGUIN CLASSICS DELUXE EDITION

MARQUIS DE SADE   Philosophy in the Boudoir

PENGUIN CLASSICS   DELUXE EDITION

Dialogues Aimed at the Education of Young Ladies:

May every mother get her daughter to read this book...

Marquis de Sade

LONG BY THE ABSURD AND DANGEROUS BONDS OF AN IMAGINARY VIRTUE AND A DISGUSTING RELIGION: IMITATE ARDENT EUGÉNIE. DE-STROY, TRAMPLE, AS SWIFTLY AS SHE, ALL THE RIDICULOUS PRECEPTS INCULCATED BY MO-RONIC PARENTS.

AND YOU, LOVABLE PROFLIGATES, WHO SINCE CHILDHOOD HAVE HAD NO OTHER RE-STRAINTS THAN YOUR DESIRES AND NO OTHER LAWS THAN YOUR CAPRICES: MAY THAT CYNIC DOLMANCÉ SERVE AS AN EXAMPLE. GO AS FAR AS HE IF, LIKE HIM, YOU WISH TO TRAVEL ALL THE FLOWERY ROADS THAT LECHERY PREPARES FOR YOU; CONVINCE YOURSELF AT HIS SCHOOL THAT IT IS ONLY BY EXPANDING THE SPHERE OF HIS TASTES AND HIS WHIMS, IT IS ONLY BY SACRIFICING EVERYTHING TO SENSUAL DELIGHT THAT THE MISERABLE INDIVIDUAL KNOWN AS "MAN" AND TOSSED RELUCTANTLY INTO THIS DISMAL WORLD CAN MANAGE TO SOW A FEW ROSES AMID THE BRAMBLES OF LIFE.

ART BY TOMER HANUKA   DESIGN BY PAUL BUCKLEY AND TOMER HANUKA

A PENGUIN BOOK
Literature

ISBN 978-0-143-11762-9

PENGUIN CLASSICS DELUXE EDITION

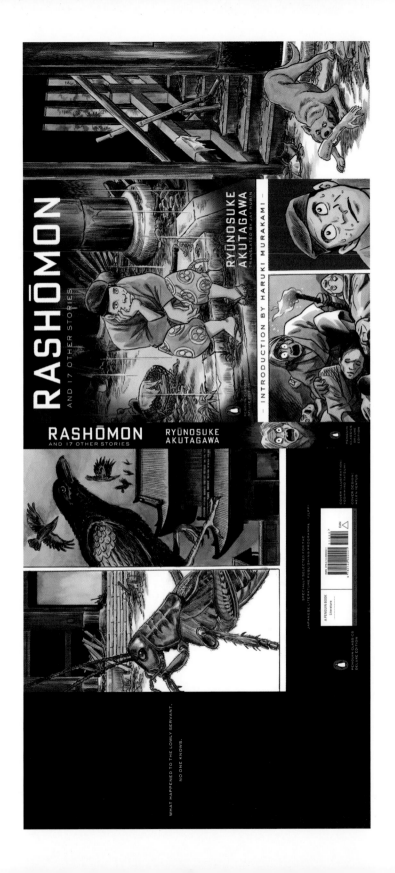

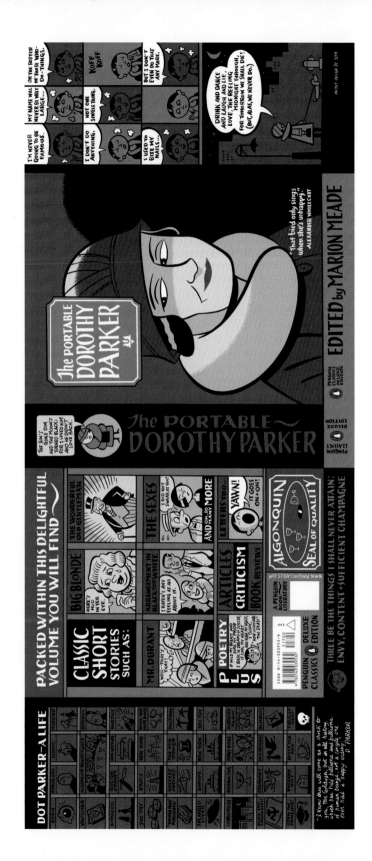

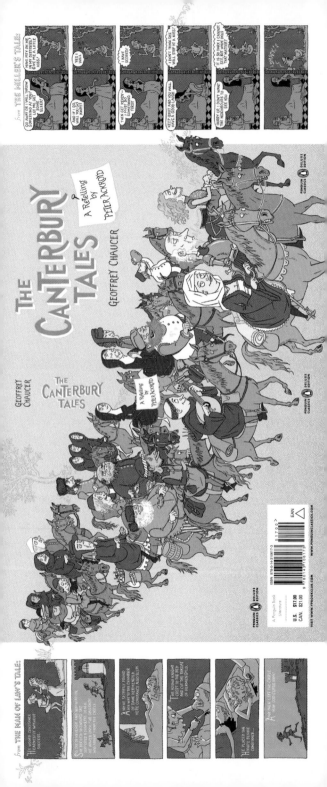

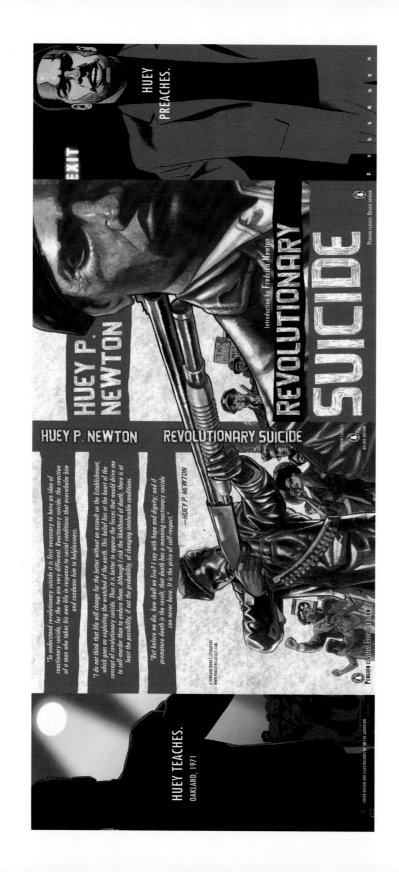

HUEY PREACHES.

HUEY P. NEWTON

REVOLUTIONARY SUICIDE

Introduction by Fredrika Newton

PENGUIN CLASSICS DELUXE EDITION

"To understand revolutionary suicide it is first necessary to have an idea of reactionary suicide, for the two are very different. Reactionary suicide: the reaction of a man who takes his own life in response to social conditions that overwhelm him and condemn him to helplessness.

"I do not think that life will change for the better without an assault on the Establishment, which goes on exploiting the wretched of the earth. This belief lies at the heart of the concept of revolutionary suicide. Thus it is better to oppose the forces that would drive me to self-murder than to endure them. Although I risk the likelihood of death, there is at least the possibility, if not the probability, of changing intolerable conditions.

"But before we die, how shall we live? I say with hope and dignity; and if premature death is the result, that death has a meaning reactionary suicide can never have. It is the price of self-respect."

—HUEY P. NEWTON

A PENGUIN BOOK LITERATURE
WWW.PENGUINCLASSICS.COM

PENGUIN CLASSICS DELUXE EDITION

COVER DESIGN AND ILLUSTRATION BY HO CHE ANDERSON

HUEY TEACHES.
OAKLAND, 1971

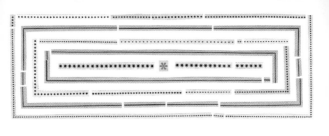

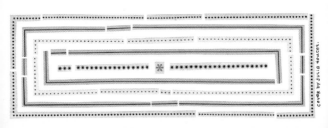

25

Graham Greene backlist

Author:
Graham Greene

Designer | Art Director:
Paul Buckley

Illustrator:
Brian Cronin

Editors:
Pascal Covici /
Michael Millman

Paul Buckley
Designer | Art Director

🗨 I follow illustrators the way some people follow musicians. I grew up on illustration, my father coming home from work when I was a kid and passing on to me every illustration annual, book, or mailer that landed in his in-box. He was an art director in advertising and a talented artist who cultivated in me very early on a love for the art form. Illustration is what I have my degree in, and why my staff is populated with designers who are also excellent illustrators. So people like Brian Cronin are rock stars to me, and I love the days I can call up someone like him and ask if they'd work with me on something . . . and a series of six books where I get a "yeah, sure" is a beautiful day.

Brian's work is deceptively naive, but that's because he needs to make very few marks to convey what's needed and so much emotion is packed into the odd distortion here and there. Everything is extremely controlled, though it looks otherwise.

Brian Cronin
Illustrator

🗨 I remember thinking a lot about the clothes I was going to have the characters wear in my paintings more than anything else. In *Brighton Rock*, I had the protagonist dressed as a teddy boy (a big trend in 1950s Britain). I myself wanted to be a teddy boy but was a tad young at that time for that trend. When I came of age in the seventies, I was a punk—which had the same kind of anger attached. Teddy boys always had big ears.

In *The End of the Affair*, I didn't want to show a naked hand. It seemed too revealing. So I put a glove on the love interest, to suggest that someone was leaving.

In *The Quiet American*, I have the title character wearing a seersucker suit. A very light cool fabric suit that I would imagine an American bureaucrat wearing in Vietnam in the 1960s. I can't remember what I was wearing when I made these images.

GRAHAM GREENE CENTENNIAL 1904–2004

Brighton Rock

GRAHAM GREENE

Introduction by J. M. Coetzee

GRAHAM GREENE CENTENNIAL 1904–2004

THE END OF THE AFFAIR

PENGUIN CLASSICS DELUXE EDITION

GRAHAM GREENE

Introduction by Michael Gorra

GRAHAM GREENE CENTENNIAL 1904–2004

Travels with My Aunt

PENGUIN CLASSICS DELUXE EDITION

GRAHAM GREENE

Introduction by Gloria Emerson

GRAHAM GREENE CENTENNIAL 1904–2004

Orient Express

PENGUIN CLASSICS DELUXE EDITION

GRAHAM GREENE

Introduction by Christopher Hitchens

GRAHAM GREENE CENTENNIAL 1904–2004

The Heart of the Matter

PENGUIN CLASSICS DELUXE EDITION

GRAHAM GREENE

Introduction by James Wood

GRAHAM GREENE CENTENNIAL 1904–2004

The Quiet American

PENGUIN CLASSICS DELUXE EDITION

GRAHAM GREENE

Introduction by Robert Stone

26

Happiness

Author:
Richard Layard

Designer | Illustrator:
Jamie Keenan

Art Director:
Darren Haggar

Editor:
Scott Moyers

DH One of the few beige covers that got approved in paperback.

Jamie Keenan
Designer | Illustrator

I've always loved things like pie charts and graphs—they usually manage to look really pretty and colorful, even when they're showing something miserable, like how much debt we're in or what disease we'll die of. I seem to remember this being really straightforward. I thought it'd be a good way to combine the scientific, economic side of the book with the emotional, touchy-feely side. And being a Brit—famous for our rotten teeth—it was nice to produce the country's first-ever straight, white smile.

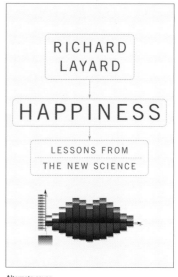

Alternate cover.

HAPPINESS

LESSONS FROM A NEW SCIENCE

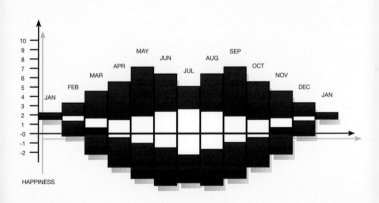

RICHARD LAYARD

27

Homo Zapiens

Author:
Victor Pelevin

Designer | Photographer:
Darren Haggar

Art Director:
Paul Buckley

Editor:
Paul Slovak

PB I've always been jealous of this cover—this simple crazy image of this teddy bear and this doll having what looks like rip-roaring wanton heathen sex. It's been a bunch of years, but I'm pretty sure it was Darren's idea, not mine, as he remembers. Either way, Clare, Paul, Kathryn, Victor: thank you for letting us get these two together.

Darren Haggar
Designer | Photographer

This wasn't my idea. I remember originally working up some cover designs using images by Mark Ryden. However, Paul Buckley didn't like anything I showed him and kept pushing me to do something more shocking. I tried, but nothing seemed to work. Paul, seeing I was treading water at this point, had no option but to intervene. He read the book brief and immediately came up with the idea of a bear shagging a doll. Bingo. Cover approved. I hate it when this happens.

Victor Pelevin
Author

I like the picture. As time passes, its meaning changes in a very interesting way. When I looked at it ten years ago, I thought about the new Russian consumerist dream. Now it's more about investor sentiment in the post-*Avatar* universe. Or maybe *Avatar* sentiment in the post-investor universe. I wonder what it could mean in ten more years.

Victor Pelevin Homo Zapiens

"[Pelevin's] best novel...his hardboiled wonderland of a Moscow sits
well next to Murakami's Tokyo, Cortazar's Paris and Gilliam's Brazil."
—LOS ANGELES TIMES

28

How Does It Feel to Be a Problem?

Author:
Moustafa Bayoumi

Designer:
Jon Gray

Art Director:
Darren Haggar

Editor:
Vanessa Mobley

DH One of the many beige covers that didn't get approved in paperback. This was originally meant to be a total repackage from the hardcover, but nothing seemed to work. After months of pursuing alternative ideas—even commissioning a photo shoot (which I thought went really well)—I like to think the publisher took pity on me and went back to the hardcover design, tweaking the colors (removing the beige).

Moustafa Bayoumi
Author

🗨 At first, the Arabic was all wrong. Needless to say, it didn't endear me to the design. The text on the cover read from left to right, but Arabic is written from right to left. Arabic is cursive, as if the letters are holding hands in a chain, but here the letters were all separated, like lonely people afraid even to look at each other. And it took a while to realize this was supposed to be my book's title in my mother tongue. The translation was entirely literal, the equivalent of the bad English found on signs in distant countries: Please don't leave your values unattended.

I consulted with my father. We corrected the Arabic, but other reservations persisted. The cover looked to me like a 1960s manifesto, while my book was about real people whose stories of struggle had been drowned out by the noise of ideology. The flag imagery of the cover seemed to pit American against Arab, contrary, I thought, to the complexities of my book. I felt like I was fighting with the cover, and losing.

A few months later, I changed my mind. One afternoon, I was speaking to a group of Christian ministers who had kindly invited me into their conversation about discrimination in America. One minister told me how much she liked my book before telling everyone that she had a confession to make. The Arabic on the cover, she said, had made her nervous when reading in public. She knew it was shameful, but she covered up the Arabic whenever she read the book outside her house. The cover, she admitted, helped her recognize the depths of her own fears and prejudices. That's the moment I realized that this bold and powerful cover beautifully mirrors the aims of the pages within.

Jon Gray
Designer

🗨 From the outset this seemed like a sensitive and tricky subject. So much so, that even writing about it now feels tricky. How do you grab attention without offending anyone? The title is great and also needed to be fairly prominent. Best solution seemed to be something typographic. So with the help of a free Internet translator, I got to work. I thought of the most offensive phrase I could, then plastered it across the cover in Arabic! Genius right?

Relax, Penguin, I had it checked.

HOW DOES IT
FEEL TO BE
A PROBLEM?

Being Young and Arab in America

MOUSTAFA BAYOUMI

29

How I Became Stupid

Author:
Martin Page

Designer | Illustrator:
Joel Holland

Art Directors:
**Paul Buckley
and Jasmine Lee**

Editor:
Stephen Morrison

PB This is also a good opportunity to showcase Joel's latest cover for Martin, this one using forlorn bistro chairs and aesthetically following along with the same smart simplicity of *How I Became Stupid*.

Joel Holland
Designer | Illustrator

🗩 Such a self-deprecating title. Cracks me up every time I say it out loud.

I felt this book needed a slight academic presence.... Fortunately, the lead character, who I couldn't stand, wore the same nerdy get-up every day.

I was debating whether or not the design should reference the process of actually becoming stupid and finally decided no. I instead focused on the figure's hands, letting their expression of "what the fuck" tell the story. And, obviously, the headless man. My favorite part of the whole thing is the void where the neck should be.

Martin Page
Author

🗩 For an author, the covers of his books abroad mostly reveal things about these countries and the way his work is read and understood there. The Penguin cover of my first novel is interesting: The image of the man who lost his head is both amusing and surreal. It also conveys something tragic. A headless body is never trivial. And, because I am a French author, the unconscious of the illustrator has probably managed to bring a guillotine to mind. It's a good cover that combines humor and existential angst.

The Discreet Pleasures of Rejection. Penguin.

#30

I Love Dollars

Author:
Zhu Wen

Designer:
Matt Dorfman

Art Director:
Paul Buckley

Editor:
John Siciliano

PB Matt clearly enjoyed working on this book and I was happy with quite a few of his proposed designs. My wife, her family, and many of our friends are from Taiwan or mainland China, and I've witnessed firsthand how hungry they can be for good Chinese fiction—it's not easy to find. So I narrowed the cover choices to three or four and sent them via e-mail to roughly ten Chinese Americans, and hands down everyone picked "the cover with that old guy." Field research!

Julia Lovell
Translator

I'm a great fan of this cover. With beautiful economy, it seems to catch a couple of the fundamentals of Zhu Wen's fiction: his surprising, sometimes scandalous humor and his pleasure in debunking China's traditionally pious father-son relationship. The British edition used another striking image—a busily psychedelic Chinese street scene—but I still think I prefer the simple outrageousness of the American version.

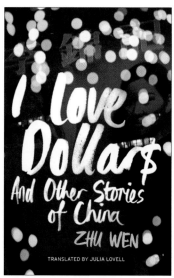

I Love Dollars. Penguin U.K., 2008.

Matt Dorfman
Designer

My first round of comps for this cover featured multiple attempts at repurposing Chairman Mao's head. Given that this route was already well trodden by other designers through the years, Paul wisely dismissed all of them and suggested that I start again. Fifteen comps later, the final treatment that won out is as much a result of the art director and editor's patience and trust as it is of my design work.

Whatever Wen's opinions may be regarding the cover for his book, I sincerely hope that he values the absence of Mao—because the comps that featured Mao were, in retrospect, truly terrible.

 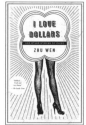

Proposed covers.

I LOVE
DOLLARS

AND OTHER STORIES OF CHINA

★ ZHU WEN ★

31

In the Woods

Author:
Tana French

Designer | Illustrator:
Jen Wang

Art Director:
Paul Buckley

Editor:
Kendra Harpster

PB Each author is different; each agent is different; each editor is different; each publisher is different. All of these individuals, and usually more, have a say in whether a cover design will make it to the bookstore or not. And of course each book is unique. Multiple parties wanting different things often lead to covers with rather literal visual interpretations . . . a scene from the story—this is not always a bad thing, but it can lead to imagery that is a bit predictable. This cover is the opposite of that. It's all atmosphere. It's lovely when that happens. To take it a step further, the rarest cover is one that relies on a visual non sequitor. We see that on music packaging all the time, but rarely does it fly on book packaging.

Tana French
Author

🗨 I'd never thought much about book covers until *In the Woods*. It had definitely never occurred to me that readers in different countries might have different expectations. But when I saw the cover design, that was the first thing that hit me: Covers on the European side of the Atlantic are so different from American ones that, to me, this looked nothing like a book cover. It was a truly beautiful thing. I could have looked at it for hours, and I'd have loved to have it in any one of a dozen forms—as an art print, a wall poster, a T-shirt—but if I'd seen it in isolation, I'd never have guessed what it was.

I think I still see it that way: First as a thing I love looking at, and only second as the cover of the book.

Jen Wang
Designer | Illustrator

🗨 Coming up with a concept for this book really stumped me for some time, and forced me to branch out from my previous endeavors as a designer. None of my initial ideas bore fruit, so I was repeatedly culling them. After about a week of this frustrating process, I decided that it would be best to leave it alone for a bit and see if anything would germinate in my mind over the next few days. While walking through the Brooklyn Botanic Gardens that following Saturday, I came across some topiary in the shape of trees. Instantly, I thought, "Eureka!" And voilà—a perennial masterpiece.

Pencil sketch for *In the Woods*.

IN
THE
WOODS

A NOVEL

TANA FRENCH

author of
THE LIKENESS

32

**The Island at the End
of the World**

Author:
Sam Taylor

Designer | Illustrator:
Matthew Taylor

Art Director:
Paul Buckley

Editor:
Alexis Washam

PB This cover came about
through a cover design
contest sponsored by *Creativity
Magazine* and Penguin Books.
More than three hundred
submissions rolled in and it was
pretty cool seeing one book
visually translated in so many
different ways. Frankly, I have no
idea why we don't do one of these
contests every year.

The protagonist in Sam Taylor's
powerful story exists in a small
world of his own creation battling
the often hidden agendas within
him and that surround him—Matt's
cover captures this conflicted
dualism beautifully.

Sam Taylor
Author

The process of choosing
this cover was extremely
unusual. It was the subject of
an international competition
run by *Creativity Magazine*, so
I saw not only the winner, but
hundreds of other entries, too.
It was bizarre, humbling, and
somewhat exhausting looking
through all those images inspired
by my book. I must admit my first
reaction on seeing the winning
cover was: WTF? It was gorgeous
and striking, but not at all what I
expected. When I saw the other
entries, however, I understood
why this image had been chosen:
precisely because it WASN'T a
macabre variation on the theme of
islands, arks, and skulls.

Matthew Taylor
Illustrator

This illustration was born on
the fifty-minute train commute
between Brighton (where I live)
and London (where I worked), with
a manuscript in one hand and the
other scribbling random disparate
images in my notebook. It was only
when I sat down that evening that I
could see how it fit together.

There was only the book, the
deadline, and gut instinct driving
this piece of work home. I had no
time to overthink it. Two years on,
it's still the illustration that I use
as a calling card.

First runner-up. Cover design: Pillow Fort.

Second runner-up. Cover design: Ryan Doggendorf.

SAM TAYLOR

THE ISLAND AT THE END OF THE WORLD

A NOVEL FROM THE AUTHOR OF THE AMNESIAC

33

The Jewish Messiah

Author:
Arnon Grunberg

Designer | Illustrator:
Christopher Brand
at Rodrigo Corral Design

Art Director:
Darren Haggar

Editors:
Scott Moyers /
Vanessa Mobley

DH I wish I had designed
this one.

Arnon Grunberg
Author

After seeing the cover of the American edition of *The Jewish Messiah*, I had the same feeling that Xavier, the main character of this novel, had while he was painting a picture of his mother. She is holding a jar containing one of his testicles, which he lost in an accident: "The painting now contained the irony of history."

It rarely happens that a novel and its cover are so in sync as in this case; both are about the irony of history.

The only regret I have is the blurb on the cover. But as is written in *The Jewish Messiah*: "Anyone can love the lovely—there's no trick to that. But to love the monster, that's man's true challenge."

Christopher Brand
Designer | Illustrator

Teenage Xavier Radek decides to convert to Judaism and devote his life to comforting the Jewish race. Along the way he loses a testicle, marries the son of a rabbi, moves to Israel to pursue his painting career, and eventually becomes something along the lines of a modern-day Hitler.

There are a couple of references in the story about the Messiah appearing in the form of a pelican, so eventually I ended up with the idea of slapping a giant beak on the Iron Eagle.

The
Jewish
Messiah

Arnon
Grunberg

A NOVEL

"A farce of
nuclear proportions."
—VANITY FAIR

#34

Junky

Author:
William S. Burroughs

Designer | Illustrator:
Neil Powell

Art Director:
Paul Buckley

Editor:
Paul Slovak

Proposed cover. Designer: Gregg Kulick.

Neil Powell
Designer | Illustrator

💬 I remember first getting the assignment from Paul. I was both excited and intimidated. It's not often you get a chance to design the fiftieth-anniversary edition cover for one of the most important literary works of the twentieth century. I was worried I would fall short of the task. I think I psyched myself out in the beginning. I came up with the selected cover in just a few minutes of thinking about it. It was my first idea. I sketched it out and really liked it. There was both sadness and wit, which I thought nailed the sentiment of the book. However, I dismissed it almost as quickly as I rendered it because I didn't believe it could come that easily. I set it aside and spent the better part of a week trying to come up with something I thought was stronger. Eventually, I came up with some alts that I liked, but none as much as this one.

Proposed covers. Designer | Illustrator: Neil Powell.

Paul Buckley
Art Director

💬 I thought this was as good an opportunity as any to illustrate the subjective nature of book covers.

I'm a big fan of Neil Powell's *Junky* cover, and when William Burroughs's *Queer* recently came around for its twenty-fifth anniversary, I passed that on to Gregg Kulick to design, who I thought would approach the cover with a similar yet slightly different aesthetic—which I think he achieved beautifully. The Penguin team really loved what Gregg did and excitedly sent it off to the same individuals who had previously approved *Junky*.

Though they respected it as a piece of art, they rejected it as a cover, and then went on to eliminate the next three cover proposals by Gregg. While one author can occasionally be hard to please, two or more usually proves to be a significant hurdle.

I suppose this also illustrates the subjective nature of art direction as well . . . knowing what a beautiful job he did on *Junky*, why I didn't just right off give *Queer* to Neil Powell to do is a mystery. Maybe there's still time to see if he's interested. . . .

Update: Neil took a shot at *Queer*, and also came up with gorgeous covers. They killed were, too! Stay tuned. . .

JUNKY

WILLIAM S. BURROUGHS

EDITED WITH AN INTRODUCTION BY OLIVER HARRIS

50TH | ANNIVERSARY DEFINITIVE EDITION

35

Jack Kerouac deluxe series

Book of Haikus

Author:
Jack Kerouac

Designer:
Jesse Marinoff Reyes

Illustrator:
Riccardo Vecchio

Art Director:
Paul Buckley

Editor:
Paul Slovak

PB As certain segments of publishing branch off into a more digital realm, there is much talk about how some titles need to become more gifty and have gorgeous production values to grab a certain core audience that is interested in books as objects. For designers, this is a beautiful thing to hear, as we are always trying to talk someone into paying for some expensive bell or whistle on our latest cover. Some books achieve a certain often intangible quality where you just hold them and look at them differently, and they just feel more desirable. While it probably will not translate visually onto this page, these three books are that—three little gems that keep getting stolen from my office.

Riccardo Vecchio
Illustrator

🎙 This portrait came fairly easily. I worked myself through six or seven versions before it all came together. The most difficult part was to decide what clothes to put on K. In the end I went for a classic-cut shirt but definitely pushed the color scheme. I wonder if he would have felt comfortable in it.

Sometimes the best drawings can get lost through excessive art direction and corrections, but this project ran very smoothly and I am very fond of the typography, design, and format of the book as well (though in retrospect I would have made the drawing a touch neater).

The selection process for my portraits is similar to a casting of look-alikes. I always do several sketches. They all bear some likeness to the person but are not necessarily dead-on. It is frustrating when the best drawing does not resemble in the slightest the subject it is supposed to portray. Through trial and error I collect the best features of each sketch into a final version.

Our idea of a person, especially that of such an iconic (dead) author as J. K. is strongly defined by famous photographs. In order to realize a fresh portrait and avoid a direct resemblance to a famous snapshot, or merely a drawn variation of it, I use several pictures from different angles or periods for reference. I obviously aim to draw an interpretation of K. that is true to his likeness and spirit. But I also hope that the drawing's freshness and spontaneity can convey the feeling that the author himself came to the studio and posed for the cover of his *Book of Haikus*!

Cover studies.

JACK KEROUAC

BOOK OF HAIKUS

EDITED AND WITH AN INTRODUCTION BY
REGINA WEINREICH

PENGUIN POETS

Book of Sketches

Author:
Jack Kerouac

Introducer | Illustrator:
George Condo

Designer:
Jesse Marinoff Reyes

Art Director:
Paul Buckley

Editor:
Paul Slovak

Wake Up

Author:
Jack Kerouac

Designer:
Gregg Kulick

Art Director:
Paul Buckley

Editor:
Paul Slovak

Jesse Marinoff Reyes
Designer

🗩 *Book of Sketches* includes an introduction by George Condo, who knew Kerouac toward the end of the writer's life. Condo wanted to provide the cover art, and the editor agreed. Not a problem in itself. Condo is an important contemporary artist, but he wouldn't adhere to deadlines, take direction, or focus on the point that we intended to echo the previous Kerouac title, *Book of Haikus*.

Condo's art, a diffuse, sketchy biographical montage, worked best in subordination to the typography. Condo was furious. He objected to his art being "smothered" by the lettering and to Steven Cerio's "inferior" back-cover decorative texture.

George Condo
Introducer | Illustrator

🗩 I started by assembling photos of Jack Kerouac and doing sketches of them. I collaged it all together with random sketches of things I could remember from the poems, creating a painting that captured the spirit of Jack's writing and then handed it in. Somehow someone in the art department "extended" my piece and ruined the back cover! I would have liked it more if they just ran the painting across the whole sleeve and made it look like a sketchbook.

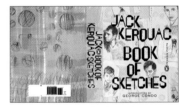

Book of Sketches, full cover, with Cerio backcover.

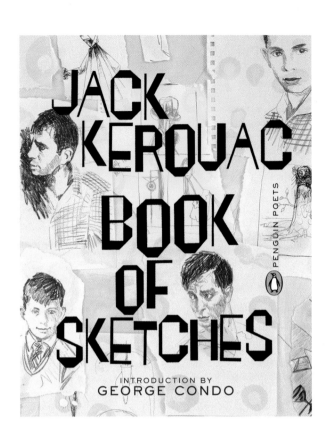

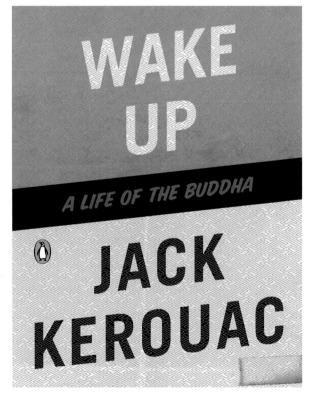

#36

The Kiss Murder

Author:
Mehmet Murat Somer

Illustrator:
Tomer Hanuka

Designer | Art Director:
Roseanne Serra

Editor:
Alexis Washam

RS I am told they want the book's Turkish transvestite nightclub owner that looks like Audrey Hepburn on the front cover. Then when I get the sketches, I am told making him pink might offend some gay people. These comments always make me crazy! Why publish the book? In the end pink won.

Tomer Hanuka
Illustrator

Illustration is like acting. You need to invest a strand of authentic emotion to make it work, otherwise it feels artificial. So you try to embody, in your head, the protagonist. Let's see: You're a slender man of Turkish descent who's a computer whiz, a private detective, a black belt, and an Audrey Hepburn look-alike. Most prominently, you are a transvestite. You sit in your night-club, ready to punch someone softly or kiss him to death. Either way, it's a deadly move. And then an epiphany: It's in the shoulders that potent combination of strength and sensuality. A pair of slender, well-defined, bony yet muscular shoulders. A glorious pedestal for your pretty face.

Mehmet Murat Somer
Author

Among all my international covers until now, this one has a significance in my heart: My amateur sleuth with an Audrey Hepburn alter ego is seen on the cover for the first time, quite charming and, amazingly, with the famous Audrey dress and pearls like out of *Breakfast at Tiffany's*. . . . And to spice up the Istanbul setting of the series, there are silhouettes of the famous minarettes in the background. Lovely! What else could an author ask for?

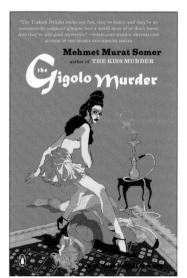

Another Somer book, also illustrated by Hanuka.

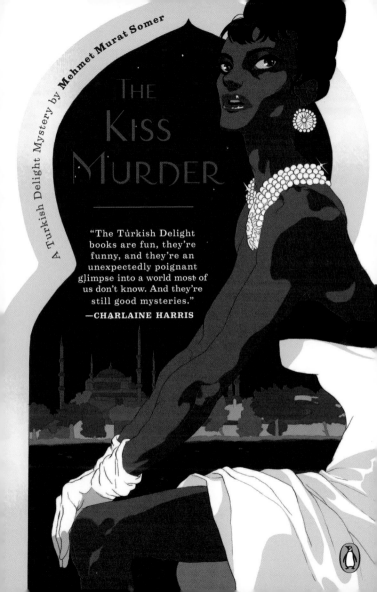

A Turkish Delight Mystery by Mehmet Murat Somer

THE
KISS
MURDER

"The Turkish Delight
books are fun, they're
funny, and they're an
unexpectedly poignant
glimpse into a world most of
us don't know. And they're
still good mysteries."
—CHARLAINE HARRIS

art research . . . and what stood out to me the most was the bold, lush colors, as well as the ornate patterns from the region's typography and fabrics. As the book was translated by a Western scholar and was being sold mostly to a Western audience, I decided to temper this more adorned aesthetic with a Western influence and try to create an East–West meld. And not being Middle Eastern myself, I figured it would be smart to keep things simple, not to mention the first of the series was a book of haiku, so that pretty much set the look for the series—spare and elegant.

The production values of the finished books with their tasteful embossing and uncoated textured stock really helped to take the cover designs to the next level, creating a beautiful tactile object. Sometimes, just sometimes, being married to the art director of your project *DOES* have its benefits. This is not, however, recommended.

and that proce
of a brawl? I an
happened . . . th
my books. I app
efforts. This se
miracle—me w
bestselling boo
gods know wha

A YEAR WITH

HAFIZ

DAILY
CONTEMPLATIONS

DANIEL LADINSKY

Author of THE GIFT and LOVE POEMS FROM GOD

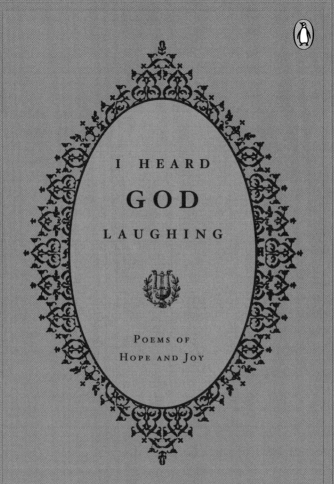

I HEARD

GOD

LAUGHING

POEMS OF
HOPE AND JOY

RENDERINGS OF **HAFIZ** BY

DANIEL LADINSKY

TRANSLATOR OF THE GIFT AND THE SUBJECT TONIGHT IS LOVE

THE
GIFT

POEMS BY
HAFIZ
THE GREAT SUFI MASTER

TRANSLATIONS BY DANIEL LADINSKY

"These translations should do for that great glorious mystic Hafiz what
Coleman Barks' translations have done for Rumi. Seekers on all paths
will benefit from the radiance they emit."
—Andrew Harvey

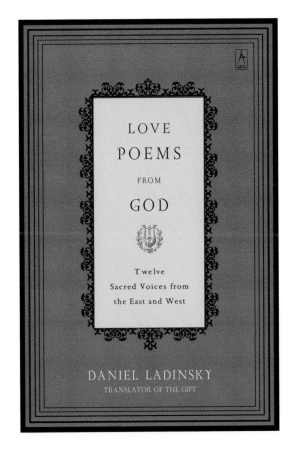

LOVE
POEMS
FROM
GOD

Twelve
Sacred Voices from
the East and West

DANIEL LADINSKY
TRANSLATOR OF THE GIFT

38

Light Boxes

Author:
Shane Jones

Illustrator:
Ken Garduno

Designer | Art Director:
Paul Buckley

Editor:
Tom Roberge

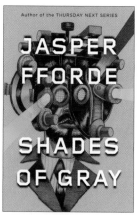

Shades of Gray, rejected Viking hardcover.

Shane Jones
Author

🗩 Before I saw the final cover, I had a nightmare that they used a Thomas Kinkade winter scene. I'm still slightly undecided about the title font—I originally thought it was too childish—but I'm coming around to it. A reader pointed out how she never would have thought to highlight the bird-masked men for the cover, but how well it works to capture and evoke the strange atmosphere of the book.

Ken Garduno
Illustrator

🗩 Paul originally came to me with an idea to have naked babies marching out of the cover with genitalia showing. It was an image from the book that he thought might be gutsy. I mentioned that I felt a little uncomfortable with that, but I would give it a shot. I turned in a couple of alternative sketches besides his original idea. Fortunately, the sketch I liked best made the cut. The characters in trench coats and top hats with bird masks was an image that burned into my mind after I read the book.

I got some direction from Paul, but he was very trusting in the work that I do. I was given the freedom to finish the piece as if it were my own personal work.

Paul Buckley
Designer | Art Director

🗩 I love Ken Garduno's work. His is a truly unique vision, and I had just almost used one of his pieces on another book I enjoyed just as much as *Light Boxes*, Jasper Fforde's *Shades of Gray*. I say almost because just as Jasper responded positively, it was rejected in-house. So I was very pleased when the unique *Light Boxes* came along and I got to collaborate with Ken on something. He was a real wuss about the baby thing, though! And my colleagues seemed a bit uncomfortable with that particular sketch as well. C'mon . . . naked babies? What's the problem? It'd catch your eye in the bookstore. . . .

While most designers bemoan having to have their gems "approved," I sometimes recognize that for me it's a good thing to have to go through an approval process.

Light Boxes. Rejected sketch.

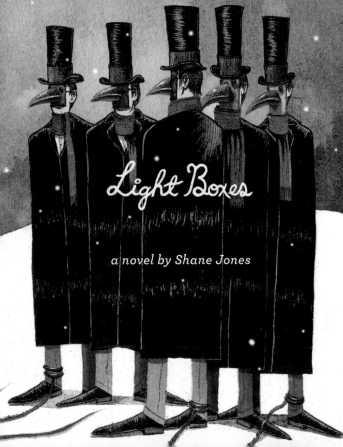

"Resplendent, and somehow nearly edible,
Shane Jones has written the kind of novel that makes
you reconsider the word *perfect*."
—Rivka Galchen, author of *Atmospheric Disturbances*

Light Boxes

a novel by Shane Jones

39

The Lodger Shakespeare

Author:
Charles Nicholl

Designer | Illustrator:
Jon Gray

Art Director:
Roseanne Serra

Editor:
Carolyn Carlson

Jon Gray
Designer | Illustrator

🗩 Shakespeare was a bit press shy. He seems to only have had one or two publicity pictures, and they've been used rather a lot on book covers. Penguin wanted to try to do something a bit different and a bit quirky, in an attempt to move it away from the crowd. I love the confused grid that you get on timber buildings and thought it would be fun to split the cover up in this way.

The original house that Shakespeare lodged in, on Silver Street, is no longer standing. Instead you can find a somewhat less quaint, underground car park. This is, of course, sad news for history. But great news for me! It allowed me to build my house to fit the type. Initially I tried a closer crop, but it looked like a bad book on Mondrian. So I pulled back a bit to show the whole building. The type is taken from a book of old engravings.

Charles Nicholl
Author

🗩 This cover is evocative and witty; it uses the tall, slightly teetering look of a Jacobean timber-frame house in a very clever way. I also appreciate the way the artist has taken a key image from the text— the idea of Shakespeare at work in his lodgings: that light in the upstairs window. Of course, the line between wit (good) and whimsy (definitely not so good) is a fine one. When I first saw it I thought it was too jokey, too "merrie." I thought: They want it to be Bill Bryson (whose book on Shakespeare had just come out). But on balance I think it works beautifully.

"Delicious . . . Opens a window into Jacobean London
and the swirls of sights and sensations that surrounded Shakespeare . . .
A gaudy, tumultuous, richly imagined world."
—WILLIAM GRIMES,
THE NEW YORK TIMES

the
Lodger
Shakespeare

By the author of
Leonardo Da Vinci

Charles Nicholl

40

Londonstani

Author:
Gautam Malkani

Designer | Illustrator:
Jon Gray

Art Director:
Darren Haggar

Editor:
Inigo Thomas

 Rejected in hardback, approved in paperback. It's nice when something you think is so strong gets a second chance like this. So much better than my hardcover design.

Gautam Malkani
Author

Graffiti is all about corrupting and taking ownership of an establishment or environment that excludes you. Slang does the same with language. The explosion of ballpoint graffiti over a classic Penguin paperback cover therefore illustrates perfectly how the characters are trying to engrave their mark on their landscape. The cover works so well because it extends the idea further than just rebellion. Printed graffiti demonstrates how this language and identity are essentially forms of pretense. The red and blue indicates that this seemingly South-Asian subculture is really as British as punk rock, while the smattering of stars reveals the influence of American culture.

Jon Gray
Designer | Illustrator

This is a book about the Pakistani community living in Britain. It's about gangs and growing up in the inner city. I wanted to make it look rough and urban, but still bright and accessible. So I followed the old tried and trusted formula: U.K. – red, white & blue + urban – graffiti = a gritty London street novel, for all the family! I then drew this on top of some existing type, to give it a bit of weight, and to give the reader a chance of spotting the title. Hidden amid the scrawl are several rude words and the art director's home phone number.

GAUTAM MALKANI

LONDONSTANI

A NOVEL

"Artful, thought-provoking and strikingly inventive."
—*Los Angeles Times*

#41

Love Me

Author:
Garrison Keillor

Designer | Illustrator:
Jamie Keenan

Art Director:
Roseanne Serra

Editor:
Molly Stern

Jamie Keenan
Designer | Illustrator

🗩 I spent ages trying to put this idea together using different photographs of New York skyscrapers. They all had slightly different perspectives, and trying to get them to work together was a nightmare—it looked terrible. Then I noticed my original scribble. The original scribble is always best.

Garrison Keillor
Author

🗩 This cover gives me a bad case of the yips. *Love Me* is a comic novel in which the protagonist, Larry, comes to New York and realizes his great dream of working at *The New Yorker* and, in a moment of great courage, he shoots the publisher in the Oak Room of the Algonquin Hotel and returns to his beloved wife, Iris, in St. Paul. The cover doesn't suggest any of that. At first glance, it looks like oak beams drying at the lumberyard, or a bad dream about coffins, or a child's rendering of an aerial view of Dupont Circle, or an explosion at Legoland. It doesn't suggest anything that is in the book. Maybe it was designed for the Penguin edition of *The Trial* by Franz Kafka, and Kafka didn't like it so they stuck me with it. Anyway, it could've been worse, as we say. It could've been fruit bats hanging from bare knobby limbs or a color photo of suppurating bedsores. So I bear no ill will, even though *Love Me* only reached 234,851 on Amazon's fiction list and the book was quickly remaindered and sold almost a thousand copies at 59 cents and the rest were baled up and hauled to a recycling plant. I still have a copy and I enjoy reading it very much. It's a funny book, though you'd never know it from this.

GARRISON
KEILLOR

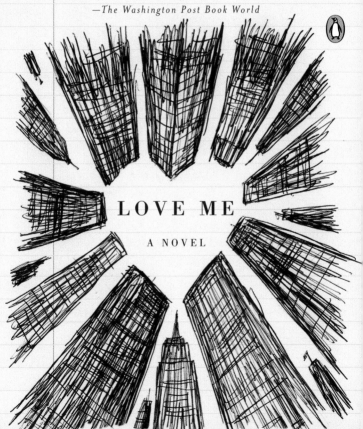

LOVE ME

A NOVEL

#42

Making It Up

Author:
Penelope Lively

Designer:
Helen Yentus

Art Director:
Paul Buckley

Editor:
Carole DeSanti

Helen Yentus
Designer

🗩 This was one of the first works of fiction I got to work on. I was excited and nervous. So nervous that I showed way too many options. And of course, whenever you show too many, you run the risk of having one chosen that you don't actually like as much as another. (This was the cover where I learned never to show anything I didn't myself like if I could help it.) Of course, the cover that was chosen was, in my opinion, the weakest. To make matters worse, I was told that they had really liked all of the covers, which meant that one that I liked better could have very well been chosen had I not put in a weak one out of nervousness. Well, luckily for me, a coworker noticed that the same photograph on the selected comp appeared on another book she had seen in the bookstore. So she really saved it for me. In the end, my favorite option is the one that got approved and the one you see here. If not for that coincidence, this would have been just another average cover.

Penelope Lively
Author

🗩 I am always wonderfully startled by the first sight of the jacket art for a forthcoming book— Oh! So that's how they see it! My first thought about this jacket for *Making It Up* was that, oddly, the girl in the photograph looked a bit like me, long ago, though of course she is not. And the cut-out dress reminded me that I used to do that as a child—draw a doll figure and then make paper dresses for her, with tabs. The image is a symbol, I take it, a reference to the book's theme of alternative lives—neat. I think it's a tantalizing jacket—you would wonder what the book could be about.

MAKING IT UP

Penelope Lively

43

The Manual of Detection

Author:
Jedediah Berry

Designer:
Tal Goretsky

Photographers:
Jim Zuckerman (street) and Getty Images (man on bicycle)

Art Director:
Darren Haggar

Editor:
Eamon Dolan

DH I struggled with this one in hardback—so much so that we ran out of time and adopted the U.K. cover. I was expecting Tal to have a similar experience in paperback, but he seemed to whip this one up overnight. Tal has a great way of creating new art from stock—mixing stock photography with his own images, snapped using his prehistoric 5-megapixel point-and-shoot.

Tal Goretsky
Designer

🗩 It was a lucky day for me. I read the first sentence on the subway that morning, which informed me that "Charles Unwin . . . rode his bicycle to work every day, even when it was raining." Later that day, I borrowed the *BibliOdyssey* book from Paul Buckley, where I found an old illustration of a man on a flying bicycle. Finally, I had been researching twenties type for another project but had found one sample that was perfect for the feel I wanted for this cover. It was developed within a two-day period based on these fortunate events.

Inspiration for *The Manual of Detection*.
Voyage a la Lune, 1870.

Jedediah Berry
Author

🗩 An early inspiration for *The Manual of Detection* was an exhibit in Grand Central station in late 2000, of work by Dutch artist Teun Hocks. Hocks's hand-colored photographs suggest surreal and wistful narratives: a book-toting bicyclist pedals straight up a hillside, an artist endlessly sketches keyholes, rows of alarm clocks blossom in a tilled field. But it wasn't the photographs alone—it was their presence in that vibrant civic space, a sublime meeting of the practical and the fantastic. Tal Goretsky's cover design exists in that same confluence: It's visionary yet concrete, like a dream made tangible.

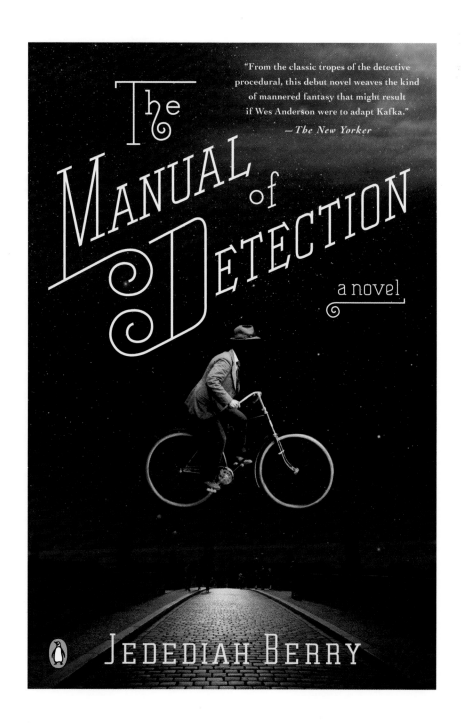

44

Mao Zedong

Author:
Jonathan Spence

Designer:
Jasmine Lee

Illustrator:
Unknown

Art Director:
Roseanne Serra

Editor:
Carolyn Carlson

Jonathan Spence
Author

💬 For the original cover of my Mao book, and for most foreign editions, Mao's portrait loomed large or even huge, as it did throughout China when he was alive, and even now that he is safely dead. The Penguin edition completely altered that concept, by making Mao a tiny figure, in his olive green army uniform, strolling across a sea of ochre. His plump face is dwarfed by the letters of his name, looming so massively above him that he seems about to be crushed by his own weight. And that simple word—"MAO"—is simply too large for the book's jacket. It bursts the bounds of the possible, the M and the O both unfinished, with two stars winking mischievously. A touch of brocade at the bottom is playful—and is Mao skipping? It almost looks like that. And turn the book over—yes, there he is again—only this time there are three of him! (As if one was not enough!) Definitely one of my favorite covers.

Jasmine Lee
Designer

💬 When I was designing *Mao Zedong*, I was both nervous and excited. Mao was such a common topic with lots of references out there, including a very nice cover Peter Mendelsund had just recently designed. That cover inspired me to create my own propaganda poster–style cover. I let the type run off the page so as to scream "MAO!" and threw in a few stars, some bright colors, and, of course, Chairman Mao himself.

MAO
Zedong

★ *a life* ★

JONATHAN SPENCE
author of *The Death of Woman Wang*

45

A Map of Home

Author:
Randa Jarrar

Designer | Illustrator:
Jaya Miceli

Art Director:
Roseanne Serra

Editor:
Alexis Washam

Randa Jarrar
Author

🗩 I've always been sensitive to the Orientalist imagery that graces most Arab or Muslim writers' books. For my own novel, I did not want a silly Eastern-looking font or bathroom-tile geometric designs. The first cover shown to me had a beautiful font, bold, vivid colors, and none of the imagery that makes me cringe, and Nidali, the protagonist, was riding a bicycle . . . but she was wearing a veil, something she hadn't worn in the novel. I was shaken. Thankfully, the veil was removed, literally, and Nidali now fiercely rides her bicycle east of the map behind her. In this incarnation, the cover is most surprisingly everything I had hoped for: It indicates youth and movement without clichéd imagery. And it tickles me that, like Nidali, the cover also went through a journey before it reached its final home.

Jaya Miceli
Designer | Illustrator

🗩 The original illustration (below) with the veil reminds me of mother superior on wheels. The author's suggestion to remove the veil was, in this case, helpful to the success of the design.

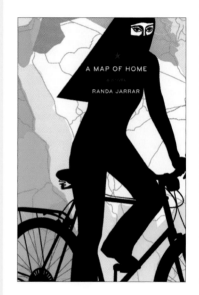

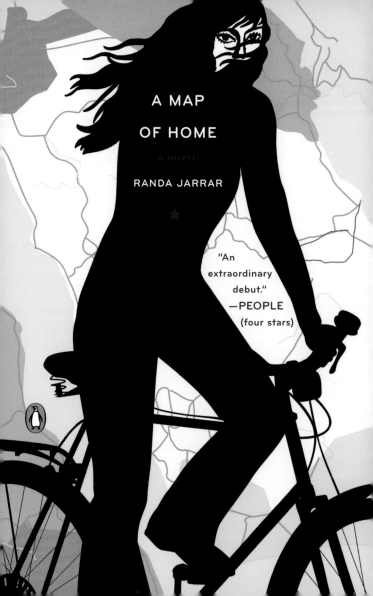

A MAP

OF HOME

A NOVEL

RANDA JARRAR

"An
extraordinary
debut."
—PEOPLE
(four stars)

#46

The Memory Keeper's Daughter

Author:
Kim Edwards

Designer:
Greg Mollica

Photographer:
Liz Magic Laser

Art Director:
Paul Buckley

Editor:
Pamela Dorman

Kim Edwards
Author

🗩 The cover for *The Memory Keeper's Daughter* arrived by e-mail attachment, the delicate white dress floating against the dark background, snowflakes drifting faintly, evoking a sense of loss and mystery. I loved it immediately—the visual allusion to the metaphor of photography, the haunting image of an empty dress. Readers loved it, too, around the country and around the world. A bookstore in Houston replicated the cover to fill their storefront window; in a train station in Italy, I stood next to a poster reproduction nearly as tall as I am. Everywhere I went on tour, readers spoke about this cover's subtle power, its beauty.

Greg Mollica
Designer

🗩 On my way to Penguin one morning, during the height of *The Memory Keeper's* phenomenal popularity, I counted five people reading the book in my subway car alone. As a cover designer, it's always nice to see your covers out there in the world, but five?! Hallucination due to sleep deprivation was the only explanation.

Never did I think the white floating dress would become such an icon. Thanks to Kim Edwards's beautiful, arresting story, it did—and it's still front and center at every bookstore.

Paul Buckley
Art Director

🗩 There is a big difference working on the cover for a book with massive expectations. While we knew this was going to do very well, we did not know it was going to do *this* well. It became absolutely huge. I have one editor who likes to say to me about certain titles, "Paul, I'm telling you right now—*THIS ONE* is going to be very very very difficult to nail." Translation: I'll need to see a hundred cover comps, and I'm not picking one till UPS is banging on the door. One might as well add, "And don't go being brilliant right out of the gate cause I'm not gonna bite for a few months yet." Luckily, we did not hear any statements like this during the creation of this jacket, which is why I think we entertained Greg's saying, "Let's do a photoshoot for this one," and Greg and Liz saying, "Yeah, an empty dress just floating over a snowy scene." What a memorable jacket.

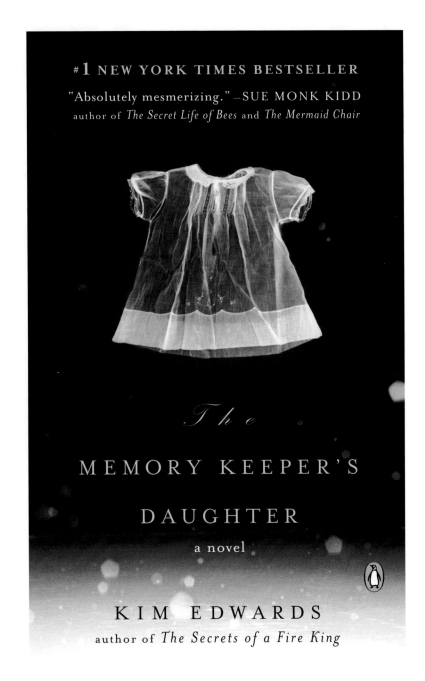

#1 NEW YORK TIMES BESTSELLER

"Absolutely mesmerizing." –SUE MONK KIDD

author of *The Secret Life of Bees* and *The Mermaid Chair*

The

MEMORY KEEPER'S

DAUGHTER

a novel

KIM EDWARDS

author of *The Secrets of a Fire King*

47

Mr Phillips

Author:
John Lanchester

Designer:
Dwayne Dobson for
Dinnick & Howells
Agency

Art Director:
Roseanne Serra

Editor:
Marian Wood

RS The first set of comps submitted were just okay, and the Penguin team wanted to do something very different for the paperback, as the hardcover didn't sell too well. I asked D&H to start fresh; to take it to a different level; make it fun. They were not thrilled, and I met with some resistance as we all wondered: Just how do you make light about a guy losing his job and not telling his family for a year? Finally they sent me back the mannequin comps, then the editor weighed in. She was a bit conservative, and not willing to go out on a limb with this offbeat cover, so it sat for months while we fought with her to send it to the author. In the end, sales weighed in and liked it, so we used it. I don't think the paperback sold so well, either—was it the cover? Well . . . that's always the question, isn't it?

Dwayne Dobson
Designer

🗩 Our first cover represented Mr Phillips's consequential place of unemployment. A bowler hat and briefcase on a lonely park bench.

Disappointingly, this direction was overlooked. Ironically, though, the same photo was utilized for what would be Faber's release of the same title years later.

The further concepts were sent along with: "Please find enclosed more concept designs for *Mr Phillips* . . . I hope you are able to convince your people that this concept is the way to go."

Final: The design intent of using women mannequin heads set on top of accounting ledger paper is intended to personify the main character's sexual objectification of women along with an obsession with numerical calculations.

John Lanchester
Author

🗩 My main sensation, looking at this cover, is of amnesia. I don't remember anything about it, or the process of arriving at it. My editor, Marian Wood, tells me that there was a biggish argument about an earlier version of the cover featuring naked mannequins; it was felt that while strong, it was too alienating and confrontational, but it functioned as the starting point for this cover, which (I'm told) was seen as a success. Seen cold, ten years on, I think it's a very good cover, though I'm not at all sure it fits my book.

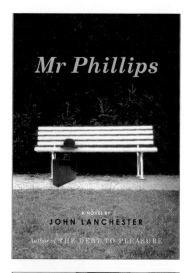

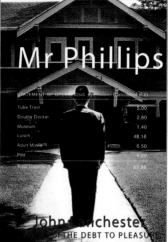

Proposed covers.

Mr Phillips

25%   55%

35%   85%

92%   70%

A NOVEL BY

 JOHN LANCHESTER

Author of THE DEBT TO PLEASURE

"Imagine Virginia Woolf's *Mrs. Dalloway* with a middle-aged man obsessed with short skirts and what they conceal." —*USA Today*

48

My Little Blue Dress

Author:
Bruno Maddox

Designer:
Evan Gaffney

Illustrator:
Unknown

Art Director:
Paul Buckley

Editor:
Molly Stern

Sorry, Evan . . .

Evan Gaffney
Designer

💬 I was quite surprised when I ripped open the signature puffy, white, nonrecyclable envelope from Penguin with finals for *MLBD*. Although I honored their request to make the cover funnier by creating multiple "A Novel" lines, Penguin added the enormous banner held up by little birds containing a *New York Times* Notable Book line. The thing sort of takes over, doesn't it? It's one joke too many on a cover full of small, humorous touches. This novel is the story of a desperate writer desperately writing a fake memoir to impress a doubtful girlfriend. The pasted-on dress, ripped cover, scratched-out words, and haphazardly chosen typefaces are all actions that could have been executed on the cluttered desk of said desperate writer, late at night, with a pen, scissors, and bottle of bourbon, trying his best to make something "real." Desperate, lovesick writers don't import banners from CDs of historical clip art, scale them in Quark 3.whatever and create "type on a path." I wanted so much to laugh, but I could only cry. . . .

Bruno Maddox
Author

💬 I couldn't have been happier when I first saw the cover to my 2001 novel, *My Little Blue Dress*. If you haven't read it, the book's a love story hidden inside a fake memoir hidden inside a . . . I forget, actually. It's the kind of thing that was very fashionable back then. Anyway, the cover perfectly captured the various interwoven layers of epistemological bogosity I was attempting—better, in many ways, than the actual book did. As one reviewer puts it aptly on my Amazon page, "I'm giving this book one star, but that's only because of its awesome cover!"

my little blue dress

a Novel

Bruno Maddox

49

New Bedlam

Author:
Bill Flanagan

Designer | Art Director:
Darren Haggar

Editor:
Janie Fleming

Left: Proposed cover design for *New Bedlam*, for The Penguin Press.
Right: *Everything Bad Is Good for You*, for Riverhead Books.
Designer on both: Jamie Keenan.

Bill Flanagan
Author

🗨 *New Bedlam* is a comic novel about an eccentric family who owned the worst cable TV channels in the world and lived in the town of New Bedlam, Rhode Island. The art director, Darren Haggar, presented a cover I loved—a sketch of a man with a TV for a head. I couldn't have been happier. Then my novel got delayed six months and I was shocked to walk into a bookstore and see MY cover on another book. When I protested, Darren said, "Oh, I figured your book was dead." Just what an author needs to hear! I then suggested a design combining little houses from a model train set with a bunch of TV remote controls stood upright to look like buildings. No one liked that idea. Darren then proposed a plastic dog (or was it a cow?) in front of a red barn. He no doubt figured that Rhode Island was rural, like Vermont. In fact, it is much more like New Jersey. I said, "How about a lobster claw—very Rhode Island—in a business suit holding a TV remote?" What came back became the cover of *New Bedlam*, except somehow the TV remote got left out. When I mentioned that, my editor told me, "Everybody LOVES this—let's not mess with it," which translates into "Sit down and shut up." The cover certainly was striking, but whenever I went anywhere to promote it, people asked me what the lobster had to do with the book. One woman told me that the claw in the sleeve along with the title made her think it was a horror story. The speculation continued online, where one reader explained the cover this way: "It's a book about media bottom feeders." Needless to say, I started using that line immediately.

Darren Haggar
Designer | Art Director

🗨 We had a cover for *New Bedlam*, and then we didn't. I originally had Jamie Keenan working on this one, and what he supplied got approved. Then the book was put on hold, and a few months later I notice our approved cover sitting at the printer, but with a different title and author name. Seems Keenan, unsure whether the project was happening or not, repurposed his design for a Riverhead book. Lesson learned— make sure freelancers know the status of their cover designs!

The final cover came about with the help of the author. He suggested the lobster claws, and I put this together using stock art.

"A biting and hilarious satire of the pressure-filled TV business."
—*BusinessWeek*

NEW BEDLAM
A NOVEL
BILL FLANAGAN

50

Odd Man Out

Author:
Matt McCarthy

Designer:
Gregg Kulick

Photographer:
John Dyer

Art Director:
Paul Buckley

Editor:
Kevin Doughten

Gregg Kulick
Designer

🏴 This cover was a variation of one of the many I worked on for the hardcover. This is the type of thing that I tend to get away with on a paperback but would never get used on a hardcover. The book is about an Ivy-League-educated baseball pitcher in the lowest-of-the-low minor leagues. I thought the book needed the rough aesthetic not only because it is a baseball book but also because of the barnstorming nature of the minor leagues. It is pretty much a straightforward, no concept cover, though I am not sure if it really needed one. I had tried earlier versions using a molecule motif but with baseballs for atoms. It was overthinking it a bit. Sometimes the best idea is no idea.

Matt McCarthy
Author

🏴 When I looked at the covers of books in my genre, I noticed that most were colorful and glossy, and I hoped we could go in a different direction. My editor and the designer sifted through countless photos and found something I couldn't be happier with—an image that conveys the anonymity and obscurity of the men who play minor league baseball. The most frequent comments I get about the cover are "Is that you?" (No), "Is that player right-handed or left-handed?" (Left-handed), and "That guy on the cover has a nice butt." (Thanks?)

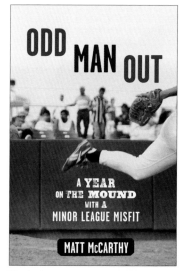

Viking hardcover.

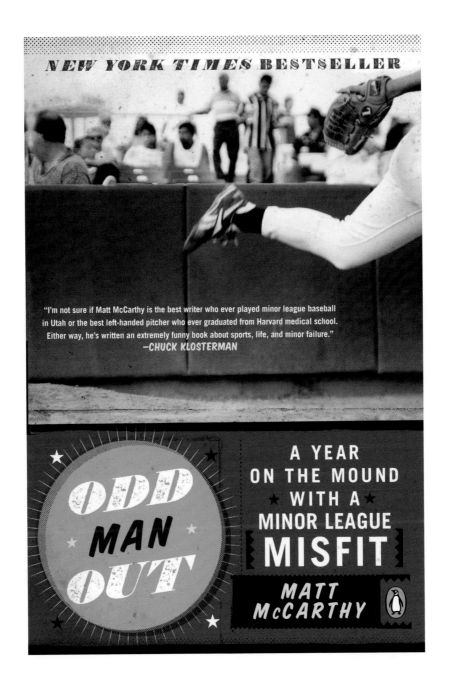

51

Oh the Glory of It All

Author:
Sean Wilsey

Designer:
Non-Format

Art Director:
Darren Haggar

Editor:
Ann Godoff

Sean Wilsey
Author

🗨 I went to Penguin with the idea of getting the best cover in print history—a good way to proceed, judging by the results. I had strong convictions after accumulating six years' worth of doodles in the margins of *Oh the Glory*, and imagined something that captured a manic, barely-in-control energy. The word "explosion" came up a lot in cover conversations with my editor, Ann Godoff. I also love all-type covers. Ann, certainly the best editor in history, set up a series of meetings with Darren Haggar, her head designer, who listened to everything, looked at what I brought in, and read my book. Then he came up with a much better idea: this!

Darren Haggar
Art Director

🗨 The sales team didn't react so well to this one. They were worried about the lack of color, and had issues about readability. We added a shiny foil to the lettering, and Ann Godoff—the editor—came up with the smart idea of printing two versions of the jacket—one black, one white—which seemed to quell all their concerns.

I'm really pleased with how this one turned out. Non-Format did a great job, and the hurdles put in place by the sales team actually helped improve the final jacket—it doesn't always happen like that.

Inverted jacket.

OH THE GLORY GLORY OF IT ALL

SEAN WILSEY

52

On Beauty

Author:
Zadie Smith

Designer:
A2/SW/HK

Art Director:
Darren Haggar

Editor:
Ann Godoff

Darren Haggar
Art Director

💬 This one came about quite easily. A sample of the font was featured in a design magazine—crafted by Henrik Kubel at A2/SW/HK. It was originally designed for a *Vogue* pitch, but was never selected. I got in touch and we chatted about the idea of using it on the jacket for Zadie Smith, and it kind of just happened like that. Henrik supplied other concepts, all of which were great, but it was decided to stick with this one.

I did commission Kerr Noble to try something, too. I'd seen samples of their work and thought they had an aesthetic that might bring something really interesting to the jacket design, but it didn't work out.

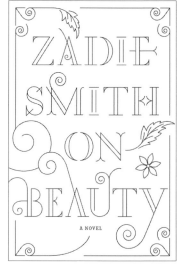

A2/SW/HK sketches.

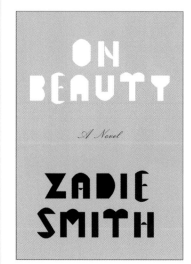

Kerr Noble proposed cover.

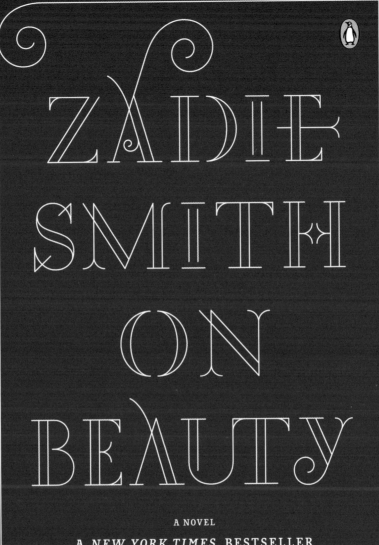

ZADIE SMITH

ON BEAUTY

A NOVEL

A *NEW YORK TIMES* BESTSELLER

AUTHOR OF *WHITE TEETH*

#53

**On the Road:
The Original Scroll**

Author:
Jack Kerouac

Designer:
Greg Mollica

Art Director:
Paul Buckley

Editor:
Paul Slovak

Greg Mollica
Designer

🗩 If the rest of my design career is a flop, I can at least say I designed Jack Kerouac's *On the Road*. For the fiftieth anniversary of the book, Penguin published the original scroll manuscript. I was grateful to be given the project, then anxiety set in when I realized how difficult it could be—how do you redesign such a classic novel?! The parameters made it easier to start. Kerouac wrote the original manuscript in three weeks on his manual typewriter, taping pages to create the scroll. The scroll now had to make an appearance on the book jacket. I worked with the very talented Ali Campbell on the first dozen rounds meshing portions of the scroll with images of roads, landscapes, sky, etc. . . . Finally, when Paul and I felt it looked just right, we presented the comps to Kathryn Court and Paul Slovak . . . and well . . . it wasn't quite what they had in mind. Overall the consensus was the package should look more racy, spontaneous, and graphic. Now down to the wire with our catalog deadline looming, I quickly switched gears. Two nights later, after listening to Kerouac audios, a few rounds of coffee, and some jazz music, this cover was put together. Hey, I designed Jack Kerouac's *On the Road*. . . .

Paul Buckley
Art Director

🗩 Being here at Penguin for as long as I have been, I've been involved with repackaging *On the Road* five or six times . . . and it being one of my favorite books, I've read it many times. I'll never get over that beautiful last page from the original 1957 publication:

So in America when the sun goes down and I sit on the old broken-down river pier watching the long, long skies over New Jersey and sense all that raw land that rolls in one unbelievable huge bulge over to the West Coast, and all that road going, all the people dreaming in the immensity of it, and in Iowa I know by now the children must be crying in the land where they let the children cry, and tonight the stars'll be out, and don't you know that God is Pooh Bear? the evening star must be drooping and shedding her sparkler dims on the prairie, which is just before the coming of complete night that blesses the earth, darkens all rivers, cups the peaks and folds the final shore in, and nobody, nobody knows what's going to happen to anybody besides the forlorn rags of growing old, I think of Dean Moriarty, I even think of Old Dean Moriarty the father we never found, I think of Dean Moriarty.

ON THE ROAD

The Original Scroll

The legendary first draft —
rougher, wilder, and racier than the 1957 edition

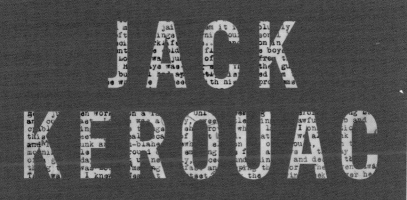

JACK KEROUAC

penguin classics · deluxe edition

54

Penguin Classics series

Authors:
Various

Series Designers:
Angus Hyland
and Paul Buckley

Art Directors:
Various

Series Editor:
Elda Rotor

Kathryn Court
Publisher

The Penguin Classics list is often called the jewel in the Penguin crown, and rightly so. With around 1,400 titles in print, no other list of classics competes in terms of range and depth and quality. From the publication of the first Penguin Classic (Homer's *The Odyssey*) in 1946 until 2003 the Penguin Classics dress was pretty much untouched, though small changes were made over the years. But in 2002 Penguin U.S. and Penguin U.K. decided it was time for a major overhaul. And so began a long and bloody process, trying to satisfy the publishers and art directors of both companies. The result was superb. The template is elegant, simple, and fresh, allowing for many different styles of art to work beautifully.

Paul Buckley
Designer | Art Director

The Penguin Classics are hugely important to us for too many reasons to list. As a company, they are our proud foundation, and such an integral part of our identity. But if we're not careful, instead of being a treasure trove, they can be that which makes us look stuffy. Like anything, a balance must be struck, and we spend a fair amount of energy trying to make the material look fun or fresh and relevant to a new generation of readers, while still looking classic and important and never frivolous or cheap.

Some of these print runs are quite small and rarely can we afford to hire outside illustrators, but this constraint has fostered some great growth within the department . . . coverwise, these books have become a really nice showcase for some of the in-house designers to create imagery in interesting ways, as being asked to reinterpret older topics and material in a new way can force a designer to come at visual problem solving in some nicely unpredictable ways.

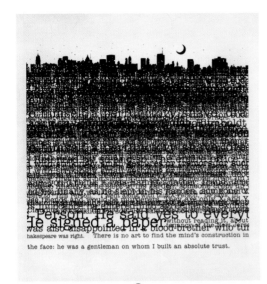

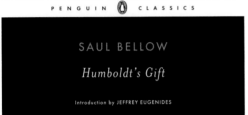

PENGUIN CLASSICS

SAUL BELLOW

Humboldt's Gift

Introduction by JEFFREY EUGENIDES

PENGUIN CLASSICS

SAUL BELLOW

The Actual
A Novella

Introduction by JOSEPH O'NEILL

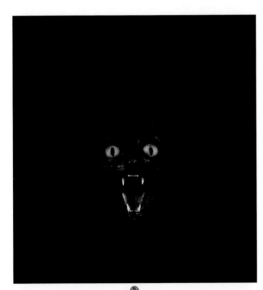

PENGUIN CLASSICS

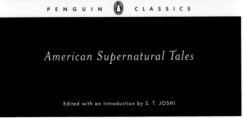

American Supernatural Tales

Edited with an Introduction by S. T. JOSHI

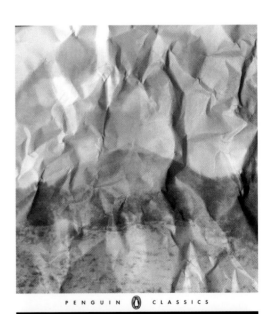

PENGUIN CLASSICS

WALLACE STEGNER

The Big Rock Candy Mountain

Introduction by ROBERT STONE

(Clockwise from upper left) *Humboldt's Gift*. Cover artist: Jen Wang. *The Actual*. Cover artist: Nick Dewar. *The Big Rock Candy Mountain*. Photographer: Howard McAlpine. Art manipulation: Christopher Brand. *American Supernatural Tales*. Cover artist: Hans Neleman.

PENGUIN CLASSICS

JORGE LUIS BORGES

Poems of the Night

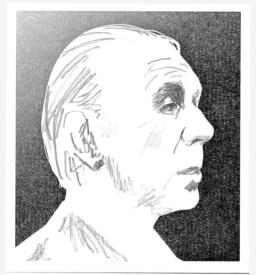

PENGUIN CLASSICS

JORGE LUIS BORGES

The Sonnets

PENGUIN CLASSICS

SAUL BELLOW

The Victim

Introduction by NORMAN RUSH

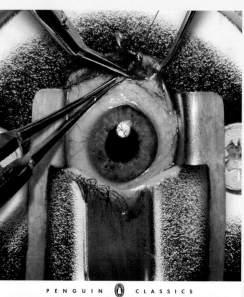

PENGUIN CLASSICS

PATRICK WHITE

The Vivisector

Introduction by J. M. COETZEE

(Clockwise from upper left) *Poems of the Night* and *The Sonnets*. Cover artist: Ben Wiseman. *The Vivisector*. Cover artist: Jason Freeman. *The Victim*. Cover artist: Elsa Chiao.

The Penguin Book of Gaslight Crime

Edited by MICHAEL SIMS

JAMES AGEE

A Death in the Family

Introduction by STEVE EARLE

FRANCES ELLEN
WATKINS HARPER

Iola Leroy

General Editor: HENRY LOUIS GATES, JR.

BERTOLT BRECHT

The Good Person of Szechwan

Foreword by CARL WEBER

(Clockwise from upper left) *The Penguin Book of Gaslight Crime.* Cover artist: Jaya Miceli. *A Death in the Family.* Cover artist: Christopher Brand. *The Good Person of Szechwan.* Cover artist: Unknown. (Alterations by Jen Wang.) *Iola Leroy.* Cover artist: Christopher Brand.

# #

55

Penguin Ink series

Series Editor:
Tom Roberge

Waiting for the Barbarians

Author:
J. M. Coetzee

Designer | Illustrator:
Christopher Conn Askew

Art Director:
Paul Buckley

Editor:
Kathryn Court

Paul Buckley
Art Director

The Penguin Ink series came to me during the course of researching tattoo artists for personal reasons. For over a decade, I'd wanted a tattoo, but as a picky art director, this decision was very difficult for me . . . what could be so perfect an image that I'd want to look at it for the next fifty years? And which artist was talented enough for the very same reason? I made my first appointment, only to call two hours before the appointed time and shyly back out, having convinced myself that this artist's gradations were all wrong . . . how could I have missed that? It took me another five years to choose another artist who I thought was flawless, and then another two years to land the appointment. I had plenty of time to research a lot of tattoo artists, and the talent in this field is staggering. And while I can't say it's "untapped," I do think it's fair to say that they are "underutilized" as far as commercial assignments are concerned.

Before officially pitching this series, I discussed the idea with one of our editors, Tom Roberge, who is fairly well covered in ink, and he thought it a good idea. Later I made my pitch to our Penguin publishing team, and they got far more excited than I expected. Soon after, they chose

Tom as the editor on the series. Using Duke Riley for *The Broom of the System* was Tom's idea. It's a beautiful cover.

Through art directing these guys, I've learned the hard way that some tattoo artists thrive on the immediacy of someone walking through their door, telling you what they want, and doing it. They pay you, they leave, on to the next person. Unfortunately, in book publishing, cover art projects can plod along for weeks as we wait for agents and authors and estates to weigh in. Then minor changes are requested, and everyone weighs in again. For some tattoo artists, this can seem a very alien way to work. Some became unreliable in the revision stage, with one artist so enraged with the slow pace that during our last conversation, he just kept barking into the phone, "Do you have any idea JUST WHO I AM??!"

Yes, that's why I hired you, Angry Fellow. And why I won't do so ever again.

It's been great fun trying to match these artists to authors, but it has also been a steep learning curve. This is not an art form of which I can claim much expertise, and I'm still learning the ropes—and occasionally getting thrown against them.

WAITING
FOR THE
BARBARIANS

A NOVEL

J.M. COETZEE

PENGUIN INK

The Broom of the System

Author:
David Foster Wallace

Designer | Illustrator:
Duke Riley

Art Director:
Paul Buckley

Editors:
**Gerry Howard /
Tom Roberge**

Tom Roberge
Series Editor

🗩 I'd been at Penguin only a few months when Paul Buckley asked for my opinion about a series of covers designed by tattoo artists. I assume this was because my arms are covered in tattoos, and because a few of them are inspired by literature. Obviously, I was enthused, but I was a bit uncertain about what the decision makers would think. Luckily, Paul bowled them over and the project was greenlighted. Lo and behold, when it came time to start choosing books and getting in touch with authors, estates, and agents, I was tapped to shepherd the project on the editorial side. It wasn't easy finding just the right books from our massive backlist: To my mind, there is a certain tattoo sensibility and culture that had to be considered in relation to the books. I didn't want mismatched tattoo artists and books.

About the time that Paul came up with the idea for the Penguin Ink series, I became aware of Duke Riley and his stunning scrimshaw style of tattooing and illustrating, and immediately recommended him. His specialty is the maritime world, but he's done quite a few pieces that possess a unique blend of artistry and whimsy, and I knew that *The Broom of the System* was the book he should design a cover for. The results speak for themselves. Duke's rendering of Vlad the Impaler's image reflected in the ornately decorated mirror is strikingly beautiful in its simplicity, and the illustrations on the flaps—the stack of Lenore's soap on one and her brother's prosthetic leg on the other—are pure Duke. No one else could have done them.

PENGUIN INK

The Broom of the System

DAVID FOSTER WALLACE

Money

Author:
Martin Amis

Designer | Illustrator:
Bert Krak

Art Director:
Paul Buckley

Editors :
Bill Strachan /
Tom Roberge

Bridget Jones's Diary

Author:
Helen Fielding

Designer | Illustrator:
Tara McPherson

Art Director:
Paul Buckley

Editors:
Pamela Dorman /
Kathryn Court

Bert Krak
Designer | Illustrator

🗩 When I first accepted the task of illustrating the cover of *Money*, I had no idea what to do. After a little back and forth with Paul, we decided to go with what I know, classic tattoo patterns. The gritty world of the book meshes perfectly with the rough bold designs of traditional tattoo flash. The first rough sketch was too much like a painting, and we ended up going with something that was more like a sheet you would find in any world-class tattooing establishment.

Tara McPherson
Designer | Illustrator

🗩 The cover for *Bridget Jones* was interesting because being part of the tattoo cover series, I had to shift my style a bit to translate to the flash sensibility. It was fun to work in a different style, though. Also, I did it while traveling through the United States and Australia . . . not such an easy thing to work on in hotels rooms! But it came together beautifully.

Paul Buckley
Art Director

🗩 Tara McPherson is not a tattoo artist, though she is certainly covered in them, and is well known in tattoo culture. I needed something a bit out of the norm for *Bridget Jones* and while I had been mulling over whether to ask her to try her hand at doing flash art, I first had to justify to myself how I could truly state this series was done all by tattoo artists if she was not one herself. During this time, my wife and I decided to take a quick vacation to Miami, and of course she wanted us to go to the famous Joe's Stone Crab for dinner . . . and who should be eating dinner right across from us but Tara. We did not know each other, and I am not the sort to interrupt people at dinner, so rather than introducing myself and running the idea by her, I let her eat in peace. I'm a bit of a believer in serendipity, so I did contact her as soon as I got back to NYC, and she liked the idea. I'm glad I followed through on this slight departure in the series, as Tara did such an outstanding job.

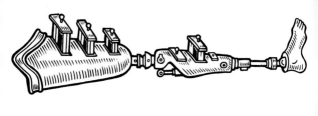

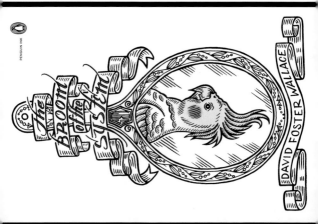

The Broom of the System

David Foster Wallace

PENGUIN INK

David Foster Wallace   The Broom of the System

PENGUIN INK

At the center
of this outlandishly funny, fiercely
intelligent novel is the bewitching heroine,
Lenore Stonecipher Beadsman. The year is 1990
and the place is a slightly altered Cleveland, Ohio.
Lenore's great-grandmother has disappeared with
twenty-five other inmates of the Shaker Heights Nursing
Home, her beau, and boss, Rick Vigorous, is insanely
jealous, and her cockatiel, Vlad the Impaler, has suddenly
started spouting a mixture of psycho-babble, Auden,
and the King James Bible. Ingenious and entertain-
ing, this debut from one of the most innovative
writers of his generation brilliantly explores
the paradoxes of language,
storytelling, and
reality.

Cover by Duke Riley

www.penguin.com | www.vpbookclub.com

ISBN 978-0-14-311692-6

A PENGUIN BOOK
Literature

EAN

9 780143 116926

5 1 6 0 0

PENGUIN INK

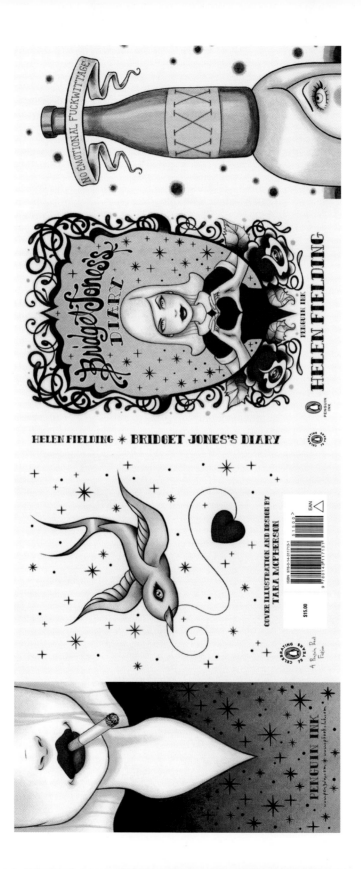

56

Penguin Poets series

**Unrelated Individuals Forming
a Group Waiting to Cross**

Author:
Mark Yakich

Designer:
Brian Rea

Illustrator:
Robert Weinstock

Art Director:
Margaret Payette

Editor:
Paul Slovak

Margaret Payette
Art Director

I've been art directing the Penguin Poets series for quite a while and have been a part of many a push and pull between poets, illustrators, and designers. That's why it still amazes me when I catch a glimpse of this cover on a bookself or in a bookstore and remember how everything came together so easily to produce such a great cover.

I had gotten a call from our poetry editor not long after this project was assigned to me, telling me that the poet had a friend who was an illustrator who did little drawings and that he wanted us to use some of the drawings on the cover. Okay, here we go, I thought, another amateur I'm going to have to entertain. I gave the guy a call, we chatted for a while, and I had to admit, he seemed nice enough.

We ended the conversation with him promising to send over the drawings. The package arrived, and dreading what I thought I was going to find, I now had in my possession pages and pages of the most incredible, hilarious, endearing, outrageous, weird, sad "people forms." I was in heaven!

I then left the designing of the cover in the very capable hands of Brian Rea, who did a wonderful job in creating a hand-lettering style that truly worked with the images. The cover was well received and approved on the first go-round.

I find this cover to be very powerful. It reminds me of all of us living and working in this city. You can see it every day . . . all of us, tall, short, happy, sad . . . unrelated individuals forming a group waiting (at the traffic light) to cross.

UNRELATED INDIVIDUALS

FORMING A GROUP

WAITING TO CROSS

MARK YAKICH

THE NATIONAL POETRY SERIES

SELECTED BY JAMES GALVIN

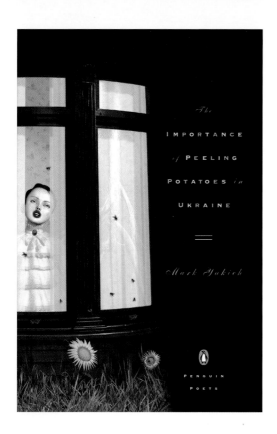

The
IMPORTANCE
of PEELING
POTATOES *in*
UKRAINE

———

Mark Yakich

PENGUIN
POETS

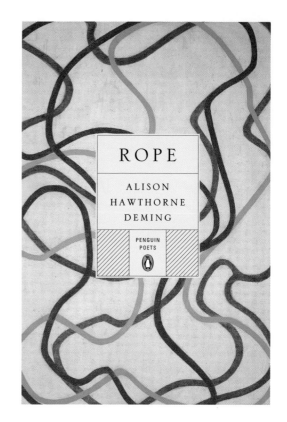

ROPE

ALISON
HAWTHORNE
DEMING

PENGUIN
POETS

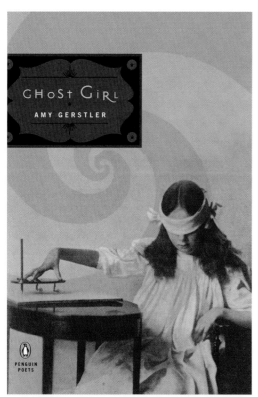

GHoSt GiRL
AMY GERSTLER

PENGUIN
POETS

WAY MORE WEST
NEW AND SELECTED POEMS

EDWARD DORN
author of *Gunslinger*

penguin poets

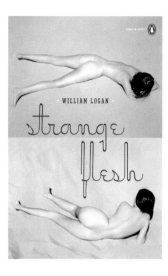

The Importance of Peeling Potatoes in Ukraine

Author:
Mark Yakich

Designer:
Jennifer Neupauer

Illustrator:
Ray Caesar

Art Director:
Margaret Payette

Editor:
Paul Slovak

Rope

Author:
Alison Hawthorne Deming

Designer:
Albert Tang

Illustrator:
Brice Marden

Art Director:
Margaret Payette

Editor:
Paul Slovak

Ghost Girl

Author:
Amy Gerstler

Designer:
Jennifer Neupauer

Photographer:
Harry Prince

Art Director:
Margaret Payette

Editor:
Paul Slovak

Way More West

Author:
Edward Dorn

Designer | Art Director:
Margaret Payette

Illustrator:
Michael Myers

Editor:
Paul Slovak

Strange Flesh

Author:
William Logan

Designer:
Mark Melnick

Photographer:
Edward Weston

Art Director:
Margaret Payette

Editor:
Paul Slovak

God

Author:
Debora Greger

Designer | Art Director:
Margaret Payette

Illustrator:
Unknown

Editor:
Paul Slovak

Men, Women, and Ghosts

Author:
Debora Greger

Designer:
Rymn Massand

Illustrator:
Herman Henstenburgh

Art Director:
Margaret Payette

Editor:
Paul Slovak

57

Penny Dreadful

Author:
Will Christopher Baer

Designer:
Tom Brown

Photographer:
James LaBounty

Art Director:
Paul Buckley

Editor:
Courtney Hodell

Will Christopher Baer
Author

🗩 I'm pretty sure there is an unwritten law of consumer physics that promises that every product that enters the world ugly, tasteless, malformed, or otherwise misguided will eventually be cool. *Penny Dreadful* is my favorite of the Phineas Poe books, so I hate to think unkind thoughts about it. But I remember the day my box of author copies arrived.

This is usually a happy day, not a day for foul language and violent impulses. I opened the box and briefly considered shoving the lot of them into a pillowcase and drowning them like a litter of two-headed puppies. I should mention that the title treatment is awesome, one of the best I've ever seen, but not awesome enough to save this wreck of a cover. I had seen the proofs, of course, and I had fought bitterly with my editor over the art, which looked to me like the rejected outtake from a hungover underwear ad. But I had been naively hoping that in the final printing, the color would not be quite so fleshy. If anything, it was more fleshy, and the resolution was higher. Now I could actually make out the pores in their skin. I was pretty sure I could see pimple scars and nose hair. And there was a fine sheen of bodily fluid buffing the whole thing to perfection. To this day, it is the only sweaty flesh-colored

book I have ever laid eyes on. Not that this is anything to be proud of.

I realize the world of our making is often unattractive, and I could have lived with the unflattering close-up of two generic models sucking face—an uninspired approximation of the violent kissing and tongue biting in the story, by the way. The irritating thing was that, except for a few brief scenes toward the end, the entire book takes place at night. If the cover had been given a nocturnal shade, or washed in a blue haze, it might have been okay. But this kiss had the distinct late-morning hue of a parking lot outside a dive bar, a scene from my first book, perhaps. This cover has grown on me over the years, but I wouldn't go so far as to call it cool just yet.

Tom Brown
Designer

🗩 All I can recall from working on this cover for Mr. Buckley was spending the majority of my time doing motion-blur portraits with one photographer . . . and spending far too much time trying to get that to work while double assigning another idea to a different photographer. The one I ended up spending the least amount of time on became the cover . . . story of my life.

Penny Dreadful

Will Christopher Baer

The sequel to *Kiss Me, Judas*
—a claustrophobic TALE OF URBAN DESPAIR and
a live role-playing game
of SEXUAL WARFARE

58

Petropolis

Author:
Anya Ulinich

Designer | Illustrator:
Jaya Miceli

Art Director:
Paul Buckley

Editor:
Molly Barton

PB If you Google the word "Petropolis," the first thing that comes up is a St. Louis pet grooming and boarding facility. Wikipedia states it is the Imperial City of Brazil. I've no doubt the title confuses people; hence Jaya's instincts to show that this novel is set in Russia and the NYC area helped at least give a viewer some much-needed context—I don't now what the title means, but I know it's a novel that involves these two places. Then one either picks it up and investigates further or not.

Anya Ulinich
Author

🗩 Red-faced and sweaty, this cover flails between constructivism, chick-lit-ness, and hipster appeal. It's sort of pink, but its pinkness is that of a Soviet flag left too long in the sun, rather than a girly shade of magenta. Russia-related books must be red, and/or branded with constructivist angles and onion domes, in order to reel in customers whose intellectual fetishes reside in Eurasia. However, these are often older men who collect World War II memorabilia, or else devotees of the undead Princess Anastasia. This book, with an obnoxious fat chick protagonist, is not for them! To get the chicks, the faded flag is embellished with a cute quote about the nature of husbands. Hand-drawn font is a shout-out to hipsters who miss being in high school. But no bubble letters here: Neither Rodchenko nor princess Anastasia would approve.

Poor cover! It needs a break. Getting the chicks would have helped.

Jaya Miceli
Designer | Illustrator

🗩 The story takes place in Russia and the United States and I wanted to use iconic architecture as an immediate visual read to portray the protagonist's journey. The onion-domed St. Basil Orthodox Church came to mind for Russia and the Empire State and brownstone houses for the United States. The author initially was against St. Basil, concerned that it would give religious overtones to the cover. In place of the church, the author suggested a drawing of a statue of Stalin with his head cut off. Aside from it not really working with the design, the idea coincided with the beheading of the Saddam Hussein statue, which finally convinced the author that the even stronger political message would not be fitting for the cover. To placate the author, St. Basil was placed behind the Kremlin on the hardcover, so I was pretty surprised by the breezy approval to have it fully shown on the paperback.

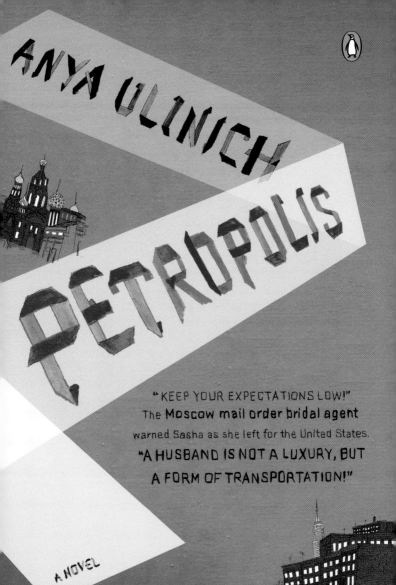

ANYA ULINICH

PETROPOLIS

"KEEP YOUR EXPECTATIONS LOW!"
The Moscow mail order bridal agent
warned Sasha as she left for the United States.
"A HUSBAND IS NOT A LUXURY, BUT
A FORM OF TRANSPORTATION!"

A NOVEL

#59

The Piano Teacher

Author:
Janice Y. K. Lee

Designer:
Jasmine Lee

Photographer:
Frances McLaughlin-Gill

Art Director:
Paul Buckley

Editor:
Kathryn Court

Janice Y. K. Lee
Author

🖝 Covers should not be too literal. Covers must convey the meaning of the book without being didactic. Covers should reflect the ideas and the tone of the writing within, be allusive without being elusive. Covers should not have a character's face (it should be left to the reader's imagination, unless you're lucky enough to have a movie tie-in and then I say, Go ahead, put Kate Winslet on your cover, you lucky thing!). Covers should be beautiful, or pleasing in some other sensory or intellectual way. In short, covers are awfully hard to do well. And I had nothing to contribute when my editor asked me if I had any ideas as to what the cover of my first novel should be, a novel about wartime in colonial Hong Kong. I knew only what I did not want: a piano keyboard (the title is *The Piano Teacher*), a couple locked in an amorous embrace, any overtly "Oriental" signifier like dragons, Chinese junks, girls in cheongsams, and chopsticks (all of which (except the chopsticks) would come to be featured on covers by my international publishers).

Some time after I had been solicited my opinion, I asked my agent where we were in the process. "Oh," she said. "Actually, what they've shown me and Kathryn has been so awful we haven't shown you anything because we thought you might freak out." Not exactly what I had been waiting to hear. "OK," I said. "Let me know when there's anything to see."

As the weeks ticked by, things were coming to a head. I got more panicked e-mails updating me about the lack of acceptable options. With a day or two to get the cover in the catalogue and myriad other essential materials, we still had nothing. Sitting in Hong Kong, I did what I usually do when everyone gets to work in New York. I went to sleep. When I woke up, I had a lovely e-mail from my editor with two versions of a cover they had come up with in the eleventh hour. I loved them both. And then we picked one.

Jasmine Lee
Designer

🖝 *The Piano Teacher* was a "big book" with high expectations and a nervous publisher. With my designs continually being rejected, I eventually found myself up against a tight deadline and a lot of pressure. My last-minute design, done in the middle of the night, turned out to be my best cover. So, maybe in the end, all the rejections were worth it.

"Riveting . . . This season's
Atonement." —*Elle*

THE
PIANO
TEACHER

A Novel

JANICE Y. K. LEE

60

Piercing

Author:
Ryu Murakami

Designer:
Kirk Richard Smith

Photographers:
Steven Puetzer (hair);
GK Hart/Vikki Hart
(rabbit); Donald Gargano
(ice pick)

Art Director:
Paul Buckley

Editor:
Ali Bothwell

Kirk Richard Smith
Designer

🗩 I remember two distinctive moments on the design experience for the this cover.

The first was switching gears from imagery that communicated the more literal world of sexual abuse, S&M implications, and the guilt and anger of the main character (Kawashima Masayuki) to a more playful metaphorical world.

The ice pick was a specifically destructive fantasy weapon that Kawashima uses in thoughts of eliminating his infant child.

The rabbit is used as a representation of innocence but also as a reference to Kawashima's childhood violence toward animals.

The second moment was receiving an e-mail from Paul Buckley saying the final cover was "fucking great." Which was one of the nicest two-word compliments I think I had ever heard for a book cover assignment.

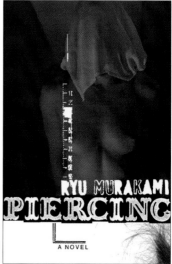

Rejected covers. Photographer: Chas Ray Krider.

PIERCING

A NOVEL BY
RYU MURAKAMI

Author of *Coin Locker Babies*
and *In the Miso Soup*

61

Please Kill Me

Authors:
Legs McNeil and Gillian McCain

Designer:
Jesse Marinoff Reyes

Art Director:
Paul Buckley

Editor:
David Stanford

Rejected and dejected.

Jesse Marinoff Reyes
Designer

🗩 The ripped-and-torn, ransom-note graphics style was generally more associated with punk in Britain and the U.S. West Coast. But as I researched the graphic "look" of punk in New York, I discovered it was less specific, more amorphous. Legs McNeil tried to tell me that the New York punk scene was more stylish and slicker than London or Los Angeles—until I managed to find back issues of *Punk*, the magazine he edited. Most of *Punk* was typewritten, with marker-pen headlines (no lack of D.I.Y. effort there). So as to make my pan-punk style appropriation more authentic to New York, I cut out the ransom-note letters for the title from headlines out of the *New York Post*.

The original cover comp design was silk-screened onto a rough stock, which, sadly, our printer could not print on. An iconic image that would snarl, "This Is Punk" to anyone stumbling across it at a bookstore. The authors resisted this, until I reworked it with author-fave Roberta Bayley's image of Richard Hell and the Heartbreakers that had been used on the hardcover jacket, and suddenly the design then became "really great."

Legs McNeil and Gillian McCain
Authors

🗩 Everyone in publishing loves Gillian McCain and hates Legs McNeil. That's important to know right up front (because of what follows). When we were working on the cover for *Please Kill Me* with Grove/Atlantic (our original publisher), Gillian made them change it at least a *hundred* times, and they still loved her—whereas the Grove publisher told Legs McNeil that if they did his next book, everyone at Grove threatened to quit.

When it came to doing the cover at Penguin, it was the same story. One of the art directors showed us a mock-up cover of Iggy Pop sticking his tongue out with the words "Please Kill Me" printed on it. It was awful. Again, Gillian went in and made them do exactly what she wanted—which was a variation on the Grove cover—but this time, much to her dismay, this particular variation looked more Hot Topic than Jean-Luc Godard.

Now it's more of a brand than a cover. It's loud, garish, and trashy—which makes the perfect statement for what's inside the book. Legs loved it. But Gillian still wishes it were more . . . elegant. Fuck her. This time the publisher agreed with Legs.

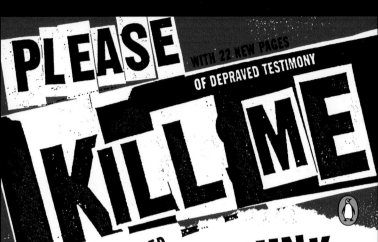

PLEASE KILL ME

WITH 22 NEW PAGES
OF DEPRAVED TESTIMONY

THE UNCENSORED ORAL HISTORY OF **PUNK**

"This book tells it like it was. It is the very first book to do so."
—William S. Burroughs

BY LEGS McNEIL
AND GILLIAN McCAIN

#62

The Prince

Author:
Niccolò Machiavelli

Designer | Illustrator:
Jaya Miceli

Art Director:
Roseanne Serra

Editor:
Elda Rotor

Jaya Miceli
Designer | Illustrator

🗩 I wanted to create a contemporary design that conveyed how Machiavelli's principles of power could still be applied in the corporate world. At the last minute, I was inspired by the simplicity and grandeur of the movie poster for Fritz Lang's *Metropolis*.

Poster by Boris Bilinsky.

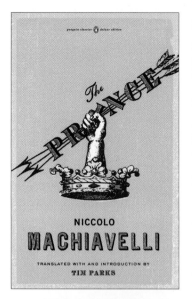

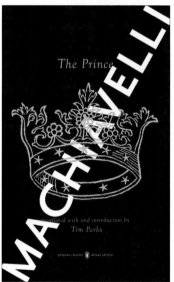

Proposed covers.

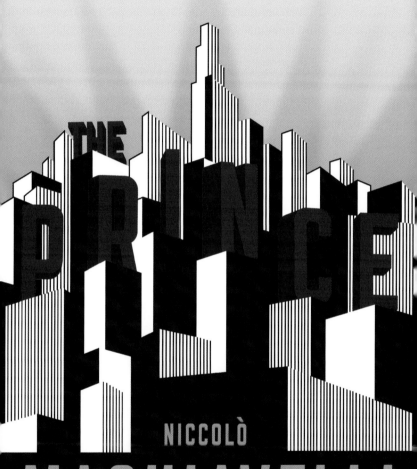

penguin classics (🐧) deluxe edition

THE PRINCE

NICCOLÒ MACHIAVELLI

NEW TRANSLATION BY
TIM PARKS

63

The Royal Family

Author | Photographer:
William T. Vollmann

Designer | Art Director:
Paul Buckley

Editor:
Paul Slovak

William T. Vollmann
Author | Photographer

🗩 It was a pleasure to be given Viking money for the cover of *The Royal Family*. I set out with my 8 x 10 camera, some film holders, and a plug-in shop lamp. Wandering into a fine crack hotel of my acquaintance, I booked a room for an hour and knocked on the nearest door. The lady within had two friends available. I asked one woman to pose as the Queen of the Prostitutes, and the others to be her courtiers. In twenty minutes we were all happy. A day later my sheet film was developed and I was happily sun-printing the best negative with silver chloride printing out paper and toning it in gold, as befitted royalty. My only regret was seeing the fig leaves on the published version.

Paul Buckley
Designer | Art Director

🗩 I was pretty thrilled and more than a little curious when Vollmann told me he'd like to try his hand at taking the cover photo for this. These ladies are the real deal—what folks tend to refer to as crack whores. That said, how can you not be impressed? When it comes to authors wanting to work on their own covers, I am no wilting flower, and will be the first to say this or that just does not work—but this image was just so perfect. Is it reportage? Posed? Who are they, and how did the shoot get from point A to B? So many questions I'm not sure I want answers to. When Vollmann sent me his bill (see the following page), I had to say, "You know, I'm just not sure accounts payable is going to understand . . . do you think you could leave out some of the details?" Due to not having full-name model releases, I had to cover their faces. In closing, I have to say I'm pretty impressed with the amount of nudity on this cover— you try getting that past your publisher and sales department.

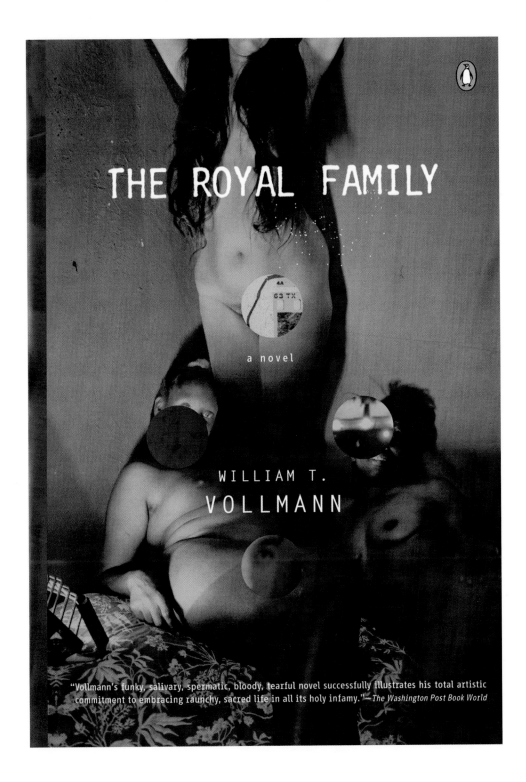

THE ROYAL FAMILY

a novel

WILLIAM T.
VOLLMANN

"Vollmann's funky, salivary, spermatic, bloody, tearful novel successfully illustrates his total artistic commitment to embracing raunchy, sacred life in all its holy infamy." — *The Washington Post Book World*

MODEL RELEASE

For $40 each, we give William T. Vollmann permission to use one of his nude photos of us on the cover of his novel about the Queen of the Prostitutes.

Name	Date
Mercedes	10/19/99
██████████	10/21/99
pussy cat.	

The 1st 2 ladies disagreed on the date. The 3rd therefore refused to write a date. I think it was the 20th

P.O. Box ███
Sacramento, CA 95818
USA
Monday, November 1. 1999

To: Mr. Paul Buckley
     Art Director
     Viking-Penguin
     212 366 ███

INVOICE

A. Expenses

FOR:			
1.	Four street prostitutes' modeling time @ $40 each.	$160.
2.	Tip for "Pussycat"	$2.
3.	Room rent for 4 persons	$40.
4.	Key deposit for room (which was in Mercedes's name, so that she could sleep there)	$5.
5.	Bonus for Mercedes, who found Patricia and who persuaded "Pussycat" to stay	$15.
6.	Public transportation to and from San Francisco: 2 x @ 3.80 each way	$7.
7.	Fourteen sheets 8 x 10 Tri-X @ $2 each.	$28.
8.	Custom laboratory development of same @ $5 each.	$70.
9.	Twelve sheets printing-out-paper @ $2 each.	$24.
10.	Gold chloride toning bath for the 12 sheets.	$40.

TOTAL: **$391**

Special instructions: All prints to be gold toned. All faces to be obscured or conveniently obscurable. All compositions to be sad. erotic and/or foreboding. Model releases to be furnished. Viking to assume all legal risks for the use of said photos.

B. Fee

FOR: One-time, non-exclusive use on the book jacket and promotional materials of one photograph only: $ ███.

Exclusive rights to the other photographs in this package revert to me immediately. Exclusive rights to the photograph you use revert to me after the first printing of the book. You may, however, renew your non-exclusive license for a mutually negotiable fee for each subsequent printing.

64

The Saffron Kitchen

Author:
Yasmin Crowther

Designer | Illustrator:
Jaya Miceli

Art Director:
Paul Buckley

Editor:
Pamela Dorman

Jaya Miceli
Designer | Illustrator

🗨 The deadline was upon me and I did a quick sketch of London, which prompted the rest of the design. Though this has nothing to do with the novel, some of my peers in the art department like to point out how phallic the two towers are. Perverts!

Yasmin Crowther
Author

🗨 Penguin's approach to publishing *The Saffron Kitchen* was stunning, brave, and original. The artwork captures the novel's themes and locations vividly, without using visual clichés or shortcuts. So many of the other covers went for doe-eyed women in veils, which were attractive but nowhere near as imaginative, impactful, or true to the story. Without a doubt, this was the most thoughtful and unique approach and is the cover of which I'm most enduringly proud. It exceeded all expectations.

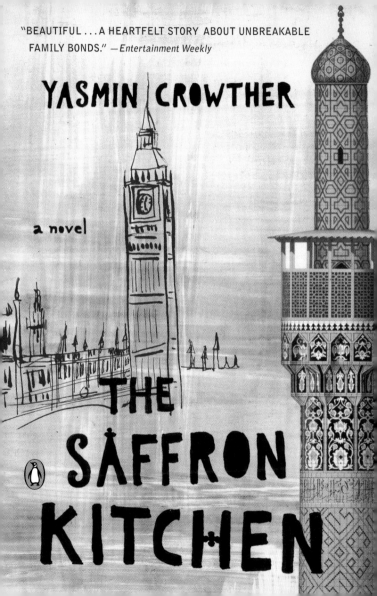

#65

The Shadow of the Wind

Author:
Carlos Ruiz Zafón

Designer | Illustrator:
Tal Goretsky

Art Directors:
Darren Haggar
and Paul Buckley

Editor:s
Scott Moyers /
Kathryn Court

PB When a book is not selling as well as we feel it should be, the publisher will occasionally suggest we put a new cover on it. "It's just not working!" I had worked hard on my cover and liked it, so I was a bit unhappy when Kathryn decided we should give it a new look. Then when I saw Tal's redesign I realized just what a great cover for this book should look like. That Tal. . . .

Tal Goretsky
Designer | Illustrator

I only had time to read the first one hundred pages before I had to start comping up cover ideas. Paul and Darren showed me the work of Abelardo Morell, who shoots close-ups of old books, and that inspired the giant book on the cover. This is the story of a teenager who becomes obsessed with a novel he read as a child, and tries to uncover the mystery of the author's life, all the while being watched by sinister figures bent on stopping his discoveries. The more he finds out, the more his own life mirrors that of the novel. I cast Chris Brand as the protagonist, and shot him running on the roof of our building. I recently finished reading the book, and breathed a sigh of relief when my cover ended up reflecting the story as a whole.

Book cover designer Christopher Brand on the roof of Penguin's New York office.

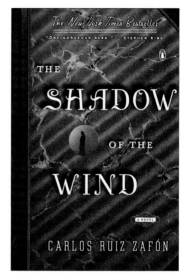

First Penguin paperback. Cover design: Paul Buckley.

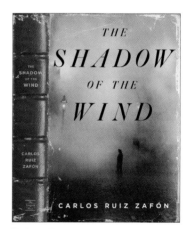

The Penguin Press hardcover.
Cover design: Darren Haggar.

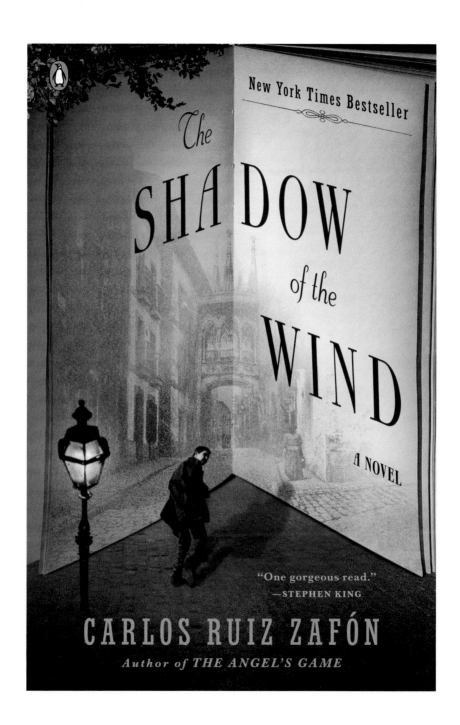

66

The Short Novels of John Steinbeck

Author:
John Steinbeck

Designer:
Jen Wang

Illustrators:
Various

Art Director:
Paul Buckley

Editor:
Elda Rotor

Susan Shillinglaw
Steinbeck scholar

💬 Typeface concerns a designer and perhaps an editor; the buying public often pays scant attention. This stack of first-edition covers, however, insists that type matters. Lettering suggests content. On the 1935 dust jacket, the squat *Tortilla Flat*, Monterey Bay peeking from behind the type, is very like the paisanos' tiny houses just seen lining the bay. *Of Mice and Men* is stick-like, vulnerable. *The* (in small type) *Pearl* (in large) is suspended in scallop waves, circa 1947 dust jacket. Other titles are stamped on cloth covers, letters stark. The assemblage of titles thus resists consistency, just as Steinbeck insisted that each book was an "experiment," each different from the one before. In the stairstep of titles, letters are squeezed, slightly discomforting to a would-be reader—"move that book down a bit, give titles more space." But crowding *Cannery Row* up against *Of Mice and Men*, with slight shading behind each book, conveys the amplitude of Steinbeck's performance: so many short novels, resulting in the accolade at the bottom: "Winner of the Nobel Prize in Literature." Nor are titles placed chronologically, also dislodging reader expectations. An impressive and eclectic stack; John Steinbeck, I suspect, would be pleased.

Jen Wang
Designer

💬 From the beginning of this project I had a notion of referencing the original designs of the selected novels but was not sure just how to do it. Some of my original ideas were playing off my ideas of Steinbeck as being a celebration of masculinity, but after they were rejected I went back to the idea of the designs from the original covers. I suppose it had a lot of time to mature in my brain, as the final design seemed much more effortless than its original conception.

Using a ribbon device (see below), my original intent for the Steinbeck cover was to create a strong yet celebratory composition in which the titles of the short novels were secondary to the main title, whereas in the final comp all the short novel titles are much more dominant.

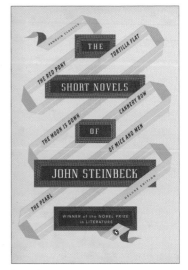

Proposed cover.

TORTILLA FLAT

The Moon Is Down

The Red Pony

OF MICE AND MEN

Cannery Row

THE Pearl

The Short Novels of

JOHN STEINBECK

Winner of the Nobel Prize in Literature

PENGUIN CLASSICS ⬤ DELUXE EDITION

67

Special Topics in Calamity Physics

Author:
Marisha Pessl

Designer | Art Director:
Paul Buckley

Editor:
Carole DeSanti

Marisha Pessl
Author

🗩 The best book covers come as a complete shock to the author—like a reader's explanation of a scene that the writer never intended but upon reflection, turns out to be true. When I saw the proposed cover for *Special Topics*—it was the third design submitted to me—it was like nothing I'd imagined, but immediately I was struck by it: the black and red squares, reminiscent of a chessboard, the diverse fonts and delicate graphics, so mysterious and strange. The disparate parts are each a little off but come together in an arresting design that feels like an apt extension of the world of the novel.

Paul Buckley
Designer | Art Director

🗩 Sometimes cover ideas come to me while I'm asleep and I'll wake up, quickly jot down the idea, and go back to bed. Sometimes they work out, sometimes they don't. This one worked out.

Late-night sketch.

THE NEW YORK TIMES BESTSELLER

SPECIAL TOPICS IN
CALAMITY PHYSICS
a novel...

EX·LIBRIS
MARISHA PESSL

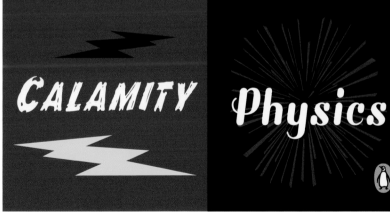

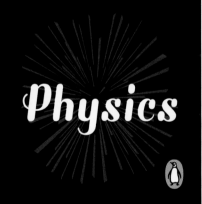

68

Spent

Author:
Geoffrey Miller

Designer:
Evan Gaffney

Art Director:
Paul Buckley

Editor:
Rick Kot

PB There are many designers I am in awe of, but if I had to choose just one whose talents I could ruthlessly poach from afar, as in some evil *Star Trek* episode, it'd be Evan for sure. He is one of the most well-rounded book cover designers of my generation. While many specialize beautifully in one look or another, so few have his artistic range. He is one of a handful of people I can give a manuscript to and just know 100 percent that I'll have something brilliant to show for it. In over a decade of consistently working with Evan, I cannot remember one killed cover.

Okay, enough of that—Evan, just put the check in the mail. Thanks!

Evan Gaffney
Designer

🗩 The short, blunt, final-judgment tone of the word "spent" instantly called to mind Volkswagen's iconic lemon ad from 1960. There were many ad campaigns out there to pay homage to, but I knew that echoing Volkswagen (and its typographical twin, IKEA) would appeal to *Spent*'s audience: left-leaning, self-aware, liberally educated types who are deeply concerned with style but go to great pains to conceal that fact. In short, the type of consumer who actually thinks about consuming enough to buy a book about it, but not so much as to stop consuming altogether. An ad about advertising—one which launched the era of irony in marketing—was the ideal way to market a consumer product about consumerism. And nothing screams informed understatement like black-Futura-Demi-on-white.

IKEA.

Geoffrey Miller
Author

🗩 I loved this cover as soon as I saw it. It captured the key theme of *Spent*: Our prehistoric psychology is driving our modern consumerism. The juxtaposition of scruffy caveman and slick shopping cart emphasized the likely mismatch between our evolved instincts and the pleasures/perils of modern life. I had some worries about him (her?) resembling the Geico cavemen, and fitting the stereotype of stooped, poorly groomed, thick-witted hominids. There was discussion about whether the caveman could be cleaned up, made more attractive, and maybe less sexually ambiguous. My view was that our ancestors, like all self-respecting social primates, probably took very good care of their appearance, detangled and cut their hair, washed in the lakes and rivers of their homeland, groomed themselves and each other regularly, and wore the most ornamental furs, jewelry, and tattoos that they could find. So I briefly envisioned a much more *Vogue*-y, sexy, counter-stereotype cavewoman (a sort of Pleistocene Anne Hathaway) pushing the cart. But the cover design and my excellent editor Rick Kot convinced me that to catch the reader's eye, we needed to "go full stereotype" on the cover figure. I agreed, and the result is one of the most direct and eye-catching covers I've seen for an evolutionary psychology book.

Spent.

Sex, Evolution, and Consumer Behavior

Geoffrey Miller

AUTHOR OF *The Mating Mind*

69

Stern Men

Author:
Elizabeth Gilbert

Designer | Illustrator:
Christopher Brand
at Rodrigo Corral Design

Art Director:
Roseanne Serra

Editor:
Paul Slovak

Elizabeth Gilbert
Author

🗩 *Stern Men* was originally released by another publisher, and I must say that I loved the original cover—a comic image of a lobster clutching a bouquet of flowers. (Get it? A romance, about lobsterfishing? Yeah, that was the problem: Nobody got it. Readers thought my novel was a seafood cookbook.) The newly released Penguin cover lacks the playfulness of the original, which I miss, but it does a far better job conveying to the reader what might ultimately be found in this story: a boy and a girl, a boat, a love story, no recipes.

Christopher Brand
Designer | Illustrator

🗩 This is one of the first book covers that I had the chance to work on at Penguin. At the time, I knew a little bit about Elizabeth Gilbert and *Eat, Pray, Love*, but I didn't really understand what a big deal she was. I remember being really happy with this when I first did it. Now, after spending some time in-house at Penguin, I can appreciate this cover even more, as it's not unusual for a book with a high-profile author like this to go through a few rounds of changes, but I was lucky enough with this one to have it approved pretty much as the sketch was presented and not have to go through too much tweaking.

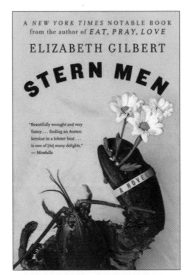

Original cover. Cover design © Houghton Mifflin Company. Photographer: Craig McCormack.

#1 *New York Times* bestselling author of
Eat, Pray, Love

ELIZABETH GILBERT

STERN   MEN

"A wonderful first novel about life, love, and lobster fishing . . .
high entertainment." —*USA Today*

70

Street Gang

Author:
Michael Davis

Designer:
Gregg Kulick

Art Director:
Paul Buckley

Editor:
Rick Kot

PB Gregg did so many amazing options for this. My favorite was the *Sgt. Pepper's* version.

Proposed *Sgt. Pepper's*–style cover.

Michael Davis
Author

💬 The following text is sponsored by the letter H and the number 3:

1. "Holy crap!" was my first response to Gregg Kulick's companionable, easy-being-green cover design. I asked myself, "Are Bert, Ernie, and Grover actually smiling at me, exulting over the words crawling next to the Penguin logo: NEW YORK TIMES BESTSELLER"? (Oscar the Grouch seems to be saying, "Best Smeller, maybe.")

2. The Muppets of Sesame Street were my muse during the five years of research and writing for *Street Gang*, which included a hellish bout with Lyme disease.

3. "Hi-ho, there" summarizes the cover's gestalt. Positively Henson-esque.

Viking hardcover.

Gregg Kulick
Designer

💬 *Sesame Street* was a huge part of my childhood, and I was really excited to get to work on this book. I had my first shot at it with the hardcover. Thinking back, one of the things I loved was the variety and insanity of it all. For some reason, the first thing that popped into my head for this was a re-creation of the Beatles' *Sgt. Pepper's* album. I worked for days on it to get it just right and was proud of the finished piece. Only one problem, the publisher hated it. So we went with a great little shot of Oscar in his can for the cover. It worked, but I really didn't think it was quite right. The paperback was my chance to capture what I felt *Sesame Street* really was. The obvious choice was to go with the *Sgt. Pepper's* cover, but the Sesame people thought it was too similar to a cover they had just completed. They were nice enough to let me come up and go through their archives for an afternoon, and that was enough to solve this one. They had shots of every letter they ever made with every character holding them. I could basically re-create a scene from the show and make that the cover.

NEW YORK TIMES BESTSELLER

MICHAEL DAVIS

STREET GANG

The
COMPLETE HISTORY
of
SESAME STREET

71

There Once Lived a Woman Who Tried to Kill Her Neighbor's Baby

Author:
Ludmilla Petrushevskaya

Designer:
Christopher Brand

Illustratior:
Sam Weber

Art Director:
Roseanne Serra

Editor:
John Siciliano

RS Twenty sketches! Twenty! Editorial sat on them for months, and when pressed, finally said what they really wanted to see. Why not say that up front? How embarrassing to have to go back to the illustrator . . . yet again . . . and what's with that lousy title! So lucky to end up with such a great cover.

Sam Weber
Illustrator

There is something foreign and slightly impenetrable about these stories. I wanted to make a picture that was less about a specific moment and more a reference to the inescapable sense of mystery and lingering anxiety that I felt lurking behind the scenes in each story, just barely out of sight. I submitted around twenty sketches for this jacket, which is considerably more than what I usually do (three). I think I was flailing a little, not sure where to go with it. In the end, the art director suggested an idea, and then the editor insisted the background be red (outrageous!). What makes this even worth mentioning is that after all of this, I'm still extremely fond of this picture. In spite of everything, I'm really proud of the end result. Strange process for a strange book.

Christopher Brand
Designer

One of the things that I really like about this design is how packed it feels. The type completely fills all the space around the illustration. I don't think I've ever said this before, but this cover probably wouldn't have been as good if there wasn't so much copy that we needed to fit on it.

Anna Summers
Translator

The woman's eyes are full of life, yet she is obviously dead, a marble bust or tombstone. Like this attractively creepy image, the characters in the book are not quite alive but not completely dead. The style of the image is elaborate, even baroque, in contrast with the font, which is exaggerated grunge graffiti. I like the idea behind the font but think it is rather difficult to read: a long sprawling title like ours requires a very clear and compact print. I would emphasize the author's name and make mine the same size as Keith's.

THERE ONCE LIVED A WOMAN WHO TRIED TO KILL HER NEIGHBOR'S BABY

SCARY FAIRY TALES

BY LUDMILLA PETRUSHEVSKAYA

SELECTED AND TRANSLATED BY KEITH GESSEN AND ANNA SUMMERS

72

Tooth and Claw
. . . and Other Stories

Author:
T.C. Boyle

Designer | Art Director:
Paul Buckley

Illustrator:
Unknown

Editor:
Paul Slovak

Paul Buckley
Designer | Art Director

💬 Sometimes simpler is just better. This is a book of short stories that have a common thread—man's attempt at containing and controlling nature, as well as his own more base animal instincts.

I'd been looking at Tom Chambers photos for a while and thought his work, which often deals with these same themes, would be a perfect match for this group of stories. Chambers decided to depict a story of Tom's in which a woman takes up running with a pack of domestic dogs turned feral. Boyle felt the woman in the image looked too tame. It was time to try something else—enter free clip art of a snarling mountain lion, and voilà!

T.C. Boyle
Author

💬 I am a book lover who views the book itself as an object of art, and I have always loved having a graphic image to bring that home. The cover of *Tooth and Claw* achieves this brilliantly. The simplicity of the color scheme—black, white, and gray—creates a stark, minimalist effect, and yet the artist has managed to inflame the eyes of that menacing, half-seen cat with two smoldering yellow brands. Further, we have a full shot of the author on the back, also in black, white, and gray, but for the red hightops. This color is picked up nicely in the simple red band on the spine. The whole is beautifully integrated. This is a book you want to pick up and turn over in your hands, which is, of course, the point: Then you open it and begin to read. What enchantment!

Proposed art by Tom Chambers.

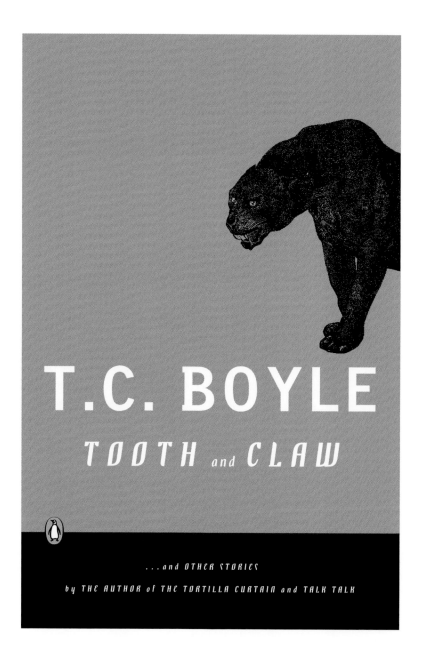

T.C. BOYLE

TOOTH and CLAW

...*and OTHER STORIES*

by THE AUTHOR of THE TORTILLA CURTAIN and TALK TALK

#73

Twitterature

Authors:
Alexander Aciman and
Emmett Rensin

Designer:
Amelia Cai

Art Director:
Paul Buckley

Editor:
John Siciliano

Alexander Aciman and Emmett Rensin
Authors

🗩 This cover, whether it be beige, light gray, or an off-white, would be a lovely color to paint a living room. It has a subtlety that says, "Yes, this is colorful, but no, you'll not notice, except to recognize that it's not a jarring white." This is important because books, especially those for display on the mantels of stately homes, should have the aesthetic quality necessary to impress friends and diplomats alike. The *Twitterature* cover has this. But we've never figured out what that bird is doing to the Penguin. Some strange avian mating call, perhaps, for winged creatures in heat.

Amelia Cai
Designer

🗩 Like most members of my generation, I delight in greeting any hyper self-aware and purportedly ironic concept or individual with a fair amount of skepticism. Thus, *Twitterature*, in the original form that was presented to me, bothered me not because it was infuriating in its concept but because it had so much potential to be infuriating—for some reason, the editors and previous designers of the book hadn't made it there yet. There was something about their approach that seemed a little too earnest and not quite the irreverent brand of amusing that to me was the essence of the book. Initially, I was terrified of taking

on such a project as an intern, blindly nodding to whatever design cues Paul very helpfully gave me. After thinking about it in terms of making the most irksome yet witty cover possible, I began to have some fun with the project, doing things such as rewriting the book's subtitle and removing the authors' names. I only hope I did the book justice.

Paul Buckley
Art Director

🗩 One Friday, I received a frantic call from editorial saying this book had just become a crash, and we needed to get the cover done immediately. I sent the commission to Jamie Keenan, who turned the cover around for me the following Monday. And he just knocked it out of the park. It was absolutely perfect. Surely everyone could see that. Just not the book's editor.

I oversee hundreds of covers a year and have designs rejected all the time, but this stunned me. "Huh, wha, you what, huh, wait, you are actually saying that you don't like this?"

"Yes. It's ALL wrong."

Then my associate publisher agreed. Then the authors blasted it.

Art directors working in corporate art departments absorb a lot of rejection from closet art directors (or CADs for short). If you lack diplomacy skills and the ability to let go and move on, you can quickly become miserable. I know this. But I also know which

(continued on page 246)

twitterature

\\'twi-tə-rə-ˌch\u0307r\\ *n*: amalgamation of "twitter" and "literature"; humorous reworkings of literary classics for the twenty-first-century intellect, in digestible portions of 20 tweets or fewer

designs are worth fighting for, and this was going to be my 2009 cover design poster child. I dug in. "Aren't these authors seventeen or something? And we're listening to them??" Silence. Stony stares. Fidgety fingers. "Yes. Because they're right."

It seemed they all wanted it to look like some old classic, the very thing we strive not to do here at Penguin. Twitter isn't an old, dusty topic from the nineteenth century. Jamie's design brilliantly married the idea of classic literature to this technology. Why would anyone choose old over new brilliantly mixed with old?

Thus began a monthlong process where we went through cover after cover. ("I thought you said this was a huge rush," I enjoyed reminding them.) After weeks of this, I contacted Jamie to apologize for torturing him over this faux rush job and released him from the project. Afterward, I walked out of my office and asked my art manager, "Judy, how old is your new intern? What does she do for us?"

"Amelia's sixteen. Mostly data input. Why do you ask?"

I turned to Amelia. "Hey, do you want to do a cover for me?"

I discussed with this amazingly bright high school student what I thought everyone was looking for. Take this info in, I told her, and let's see what you have in a few days.

About two minutes later, reason kicked in, and I e-mailed her to say, please don't take this personally, but I'll be working on this, too, because I can't just hand it over to some sixteen-year-old without backup.

I then banged out some cookie-cutter designs that I was sure would look brilliant next to whatever a sixteen-year-old might produce. These people don't know what they want anyway, I told myself. Half an hour later I thought, hey these don't look so bad after all. I patted myself on the back. Well, twenty years experience has to add up to something, right? Good job, Paul. Why, thanks, Paul. Hey man, seriously, you're very welcome.

A few days later, Amelia gave me her cover proposals, and I said, "This isn't the book's subtitle . . . and where are the author names?"

"Well, I rewrote the subtitle and I figured we'd put their names on the spine."

"You know, Amelia, you can't just do that."

"Why not?"

"Never mind, I gotta get these into my meeting. Thanks. . . ."

I walked up to my packaging meeting, and after we all sheepishly batted around some mildly tense banter about whether these as yet unseen cover proposals would cause yet further sparks today, I put both sets of comps on the table. Immediately everyone reached out, pushing my designs aside to get a better look at Amelia's.

"OOOOOhh, these are great! . . . ABSOLUTELY great! Who did these?"

"Intern downstairs."

"Much better than these," they said, pointing to my designs. "Let's get these things off the table."

"Hey! Hey, did you notice that there are no author names, and the subtitle is different?" "Yes, it's perfect. So smart! This really reads much better now."

"But . . ." I said.

"No, Paul, this is what we've been needing the whole time!"

Actually, it was a pretty beautiful thing. That Amelia is going places.

_____

Twitterature

THE WORLD'S
GREATEST BOOKS
NOW PRESENTED
IN TWENTY
TWEETS OR LESS

Alexander Aciman and Emmett L. Rensin

74

Wolf Totem

Author:
Jiang Rong

Designer | Illustrator:
Elsa Chiao

Art Director:
Darren Haggar

Editor:
Liza Darnton

DH Another instance where my staff prove they're more talented than I am. We both worked on this one, but everyone preferred Elsa's designs. This happens a lot.

Howard Goldblatt
Translator

💬 Where to start in designing this cover couldn't have been a tough call: a wolf. I loved the hardcover—three phases (faces) of a single wolf that had a Jack London feel, yet was slightly ambiguous. At first the ambiguity seemed lost in the paperback, which I saw in black and white only, and didn't much like. It needed color and definition. Which is what it got: the arresting blue and a spiky, angry wolf at the foot of a (Mongolian) mountain. Adding the translator's name would have been nice, but this tops the other covers I've seen.

Elsa Chiao
Designer | Illustrator

💬 I knew from the beginning that I wanted Mongolian/Chinese paper cutting on the cover. However, it was very hard to find a Mongolian paper cutting artist who could turn it around in three days. So I had to channel my inner Mongolian grasslander to produce the art myself. I also managed to work my own Chinese calligraphy into the design, which I am quite proud of. You don't really notice it at that miniscule size next to the title, but it's there, and it says "wolf totem." My grade school calligraphy teacher in Taiwan would be proud.

The Penguin Press hardcover.
Designer: Darren Haggar.
Photo: Bob Elsdale.

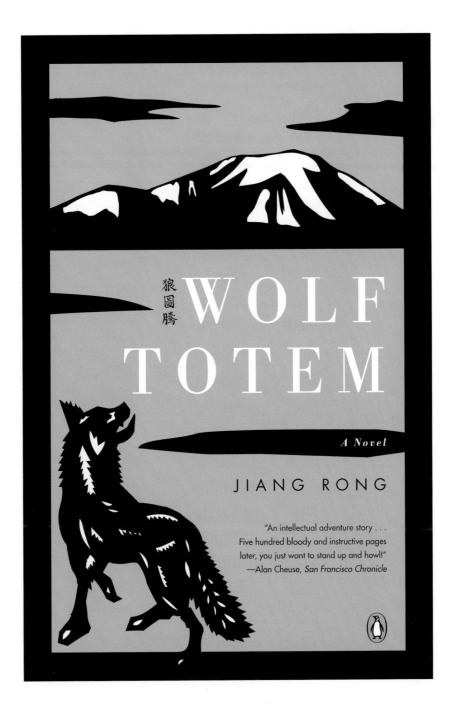

75

Zero

Author:
Charles Seife

Designer:
Herb Thornby
at Post Tool Design

Art Director:
Paul Buckley

Editor:
Wendy Wolf

PB Among our editorial department, there is much segmenting of subject matter. This one does the big biographies, this one commercial women's fiction, this one military history, etc. For obvious reasons, this editing makes sense, but I try to avoid this on the design end of things. But I must admit, every time I get a book like this to package, my brain says, "Herb." He always just gets it indubitably with ease and grace.

Charles Seife
Author

The hardcover *Zero* had a stark white jacket; the only adornment was a vertical gray line piercing the "o" in the title. It was classy, and it evoked the cold nothingness of the subject matter—if anything, too effectively. When I first saw the proposed cover for the paperback, though, I was thrilled at how warm and inviting the design had become, even while keeping many of the design elements of the original jacket. And the circle carved out of the red and black field hints at emptiness even more effectively than did the vast white void.

Herb Thornby
Designer

This was one of the first projects I worked on when I started working at Post Tool Design in San Francisco. The partners Gigi Obrecht and David Karam had designed a beautiful hardcover, and Penguin wanted something slightly different for the paperback. I am a bit of a math dork, so I think an entire book devoted to a single number is a sublime idea. I have always hoped for a sequel—maybe for 1 or %.

ZERO

The Biography of a Dangerous Idea

Charles Seife

Viking hardcover.

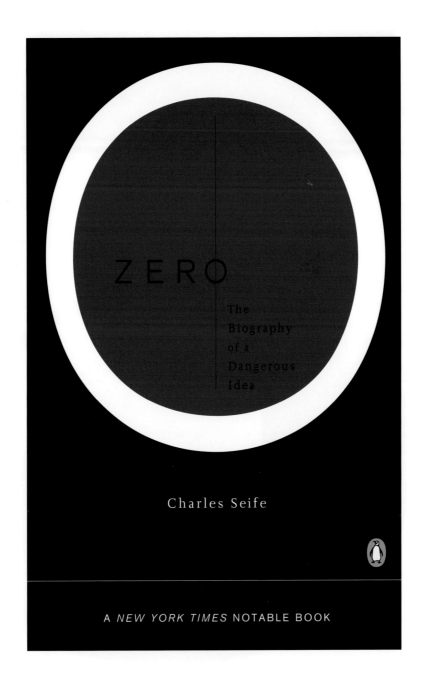

ZERO

The
Biography
of a
Dangerous
Idea

Charles Seife

A *NEW YORK TIMES* NOTABLE BOOK

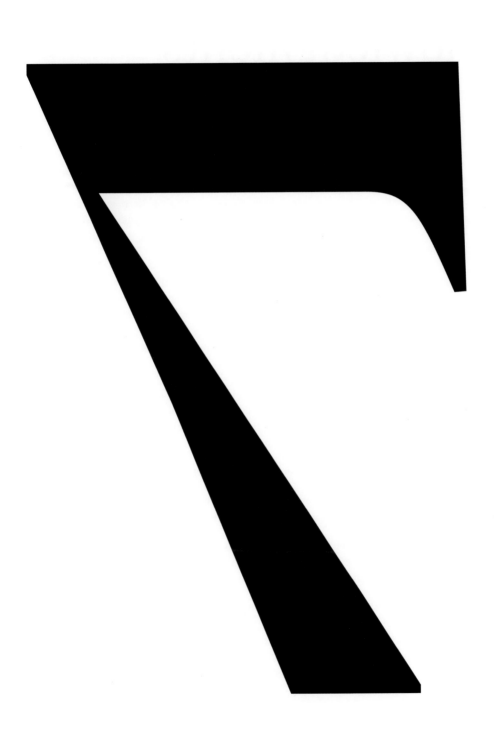

Acknowledgments

Gathering the contents for this book and assembling all the separate elements could never have been accomplished without the help of so many people. Every editor who works for Penguin, Viking, and The Penguin Press helped, as did every author on these pages—without these people and their efforts on my behalf, there would be no *Penguin 75*. The same, of course, is true for every art director, designer, illustrator, and photographer who agreed to give me a comment and whose work contributed to making this book so visually engaging—none more so than Roseanne Serra and Darren Haggar, two of the most talented art directors working today.

As in most endeavors, there was a core team who really pulled this book together. Dolores Reilly supervised the production. Matt Giarratano managed the editorial process, which when working with visual artists means a ton of work. Alex Gigante, Linda Cowen, and Gina Anderson made sure all was legally sound. George Baier IV and Cristina Stoll in collaboration with Judy Ng, who collected all the files, made sure that the art looked perfect and the many files sent to the printer were flawless. Andrew Lau gathered endless permission forms. Our marketing, publicity, and promotion departments each pitched in their expertise. A huge thank-you to all of these folks.

Chris Ware generously agreed to write the foreword—thank you Chris. Adrian Tomine put us in touch with Yoshihiro Tatsumi and was a patient liason for not only the *Rashōmon* cover but was nice enough to reach out to Mr. Tatsumi again to request a comment for this book. I'd like to also take this opportunity to thank the ever generous Eric Reynolds whose help with the Graphic Classics series has been paramount.

The three people I worked most closely with on this book were Rebecca Hunt, Chris Brand, and Kathryn Court.

Rebecca Hunt is the Penguin editor who worked on every page of this book, editing and assembling author comments, tracking down the hard to find, and making sure we all stayed on track. Becca, thank you for all of your help.

Chris Brand designed this book in addition to his full-time job as a member of my staff. For months, Chris was in the office nights and weekends giving this book top priority, and with him overseeing the design, I suffered not one moment of insecurity as to whether this book would be beautiful. It simply was never in question, as Chris is one of the very best.

And as they say, last but not least, Kathryn Court, the book's publisher, who generously allowed me to pursue this idea: Two thousand ten marks the seventy-fifth anniversary of Penguin Books and also my twentieth anniversary with the company, and that is in great part due to working with Kathryn, who has always been a huge fan of art and design and has in turn fostered that interest in her editorial staff, making the Penguin environment one in which designers and art directors can do strong work and pursue new and unusual territory. Thanks, Kathryn.

Index

PENGUIN BOOKS

Published by the Penguin Group
Penguin Group (USA) Inc., 375 Hudson Street, New York, New York 10014, U.S.A.
Penguin Group (Canada), 90 Eglinton Avenue East, Suite 700, Toronto, Ontario, Canada M4P 2Y3
(a division of Pearson Penguin Canada Inc.)
Penguin Books Ltd, 80 Strand, London WC2R 0RL, England
Penguin Ireland, 25 St Stephen's Green, Dublin 2, Ireland (a division of Penguin Books Ltd)
Penguin Group (Australia), 250 Camberwell Road, Camberwell, Victoria 3124, Australia
(a division of Pearson Australia Group Pty Ltd)
Penguin Books India Pvt Ltd, 11 Community Centre, Panchsheel Park, New Delhi – 110 017, India
Penguin Group (NZ), 67 Apollo Drive, Rosedale, North Shore 0632, New Zealand
(a division of Pearson New Zealand Ltd)
Penguin Books (South Africa) (Pty) Ltd, 24 Sturdee Avenue, Rosebank, Johannesburg 2196, South Africa

Penguin Books Ltd, Registered Offices: 80 Strand, London WC2R 0RL, England

First published in Penguin Books 2010

10 9 8 7 6 5 4 3 2 1

ISBN 978-0-14-311762-9
CIP data available

Printed in the United States of America